D0848708

WELLINGTON

SUTTON POCKET BIOGRAPHIES

Series Editor C.S. Nicholls

Highly readable brief lives of those who have played a significant part in history, and whose contributions still influence contemporary culture.

WELLINGTON

A NEW BIOGRAPHY

ELIZABETH LONGFORD

SUTTON PUBLISHING

For
Frank, Thomas and Maria

First published in 2001 by
Sutton Publishing Limited · Phoenix Mill
Thrupp · Stroud · Gloucestershire · GL5 2BU

Reprinted in 2002

British Library Cataloguing in Publication Data

A catalogue record for this book is available from the
British Library.

ISBN 0 7509 2694 5

Typeset in 11/15 pt Perpetua.
Typesetting and origination by
Sutton Publishing Limited
Printed and bound in England by
J.H. Haynes & Co. Ltd, Sparkford.

CONTENTS

Contents

FOREWORD

by Lord Guthrie
former Chief of the Defence Staff

Wellington, posthumously nicknamed 'The Iron Duke', was a genius and one of the truly great British leaders. Many have written about him but I doubt if Elizabeth Longford's biography has ever been or could be bettered. She not only writes of him as a soldier but of what made him the man he was; the times he was brought up in and the country's political and public life.

He learnt his soldiering in India and while conducting the prolonged and wearisome Peninsular campaign. Constantly exposed to great danger, he survived battle after battle before his final triumph at Waterloo. He was the most undemonstrative of men. Yet he could still serve as the model for a modern army officer. He insisted on seeing everything for himself. And he cared for his men – as they knew well. Unlike his great rival, he never put them unnecessarily in harm's way.

He was forty-six at the time of Waterloo and although he continued to serve his country at the very highest levels he never fought another battle. His victory destroyed the French threat and he enabled Europe to live in peace for many years. Elizabeth Longford's biography has done justice to her subject and the times in which he lived.

PREFACE

It is nearly half a century since I began my research on Wellington, and one of the things that inspired me was the thought that he was the great-great-uncle of my husband Frank. Wellington had married Frank's great-great-aunt, Kitty Pakenham. The family connection helped me win the warm support of Gerry Wellington, the 7th Duke. Like a character in one of Shakespeare's comedies, Gerry would address me as 'cos'. He opened all his archives, took me to see Wellington's funeral coach and the grave at Stratfield Saye of Wellington's charger, Copenhagen. Then we would argue about the drafts of my biography. Had I put in too much of the scandal about Harriet Wilson? Gerry thought I had. But he never attempted to muzzle me. 'It's your book, Elizabeth,' he would say. 'You must make your own decisions.' His son Valerian, 8th and current Duke, and Valerian's son and daughter-in-law, Charles and Antonia Douro, have also given me help of every sort.

In this abridgement I have not had much space for the links between Wellington and the Pakenham family — apart from the unfortunate marriage to Kitty herself. But for her younger brothers Neil and Hercules the Wellington connection was no misfortune. Both rose rapidly to be generals in Wellington's army in the Peninsula — accelerated promotion that would be called 'sleaze' today but was then taken for granted. In due course their brother Henry, Dean of St Patrick's Cathedral in Dublin, appealed to Wellington, then Prime Minister, to help in his career. 'One word from you, Arthur, and I would be a bishop.' But on this occasion the Duke was adamant. 'Not a word, Henry,' he replied, 'not one word.'

LIST OF
ILLUSTRATIONS

List of Illustrations

ACKNOWLEDGEMENTS

First of all I should like to thank Her Majesty the Queen for again allowing me to use the Royal Archives in the Round Tower, Windsor Castle for purposes of general research in connection with this book. I must again thank Sheila, Lady de Bellaigue for her invaluable advice in matters involving Queen Victoria. I would also like to thank her for her wonderfully kind and enjoyable invitation to me to christen the first electrical booklift at the Royal Archives; there is to be no more toiling up long steep steps. I must also thank my granddaughter Flora Soros for driving me to and from the archives on this and other occasions.

I must also thank my eldest granddaughter Rebecca Fitzgerald for helping me in discussing the problems of condensing the book without dissolving its life and spirit.

Finally, I should like to thank my granddaughter Maria Winner for transcribing, typing, and editing this text for publication.

CHRONOLOGY

1769	**1 May.** Birth
1781	Death of father
1784	Leaves Eton
1787	Becomes lieutenant in 76th Regiment
1790	MP for Trim, Ireland
1794	Commands brigade in Flanders
1796	Goes to India and fights in Mysore and 2nd Mahratta wars
1804	Becomes Knight of the Bath
1805	Returns to England from India
1806	Marries Kitty Pakenham, sister of the Earl of Longford
	Becomes MP for Rye (later for Mitchell in Cornwall and Newport in the Isle of Wight)
1807	Becomes Chief Secretary for Ireland
	Birth of son Arthur
	Goes to Denmark and brings about its surrender
1808	Fights French army in Portugal – Battles of Roliça and Vimeiro
	Signs Convention of Cintra
	Birth of second son, Charles

1809	Fights in Portugal at Oporto and in Spain at Talavera
	Becomes Viscount Wellington
1810	Fights in Portugal at Torres Vedras
1812	Fights in Spain at Ciudad Rodrigo, Salamanca and Badajoz. Is repulsed at Burgos
	Becomes Marquess of Wellington
1813	Battles of Vitoria, Pamplona, San Sebastián and Nivelle
1814	Penetrates France. Battles of Orthez and Toulouse
	Napoleon abdicates and is sent to Elba
	Becomes ambassador in Paris
	Becomes Duke of Wellington
1815	Napoleon escapes from Elba
	18 June. Wellington defeats him at Battle of Waterloo
1818	Joins Lord Liverpool's Tory Cabinet as Master-General of Ordnance
1827	Refuses to join Cabinet of new Tory PM, George Canning
1828	**9 January.** Becomes Prime Minister
1829	Enacts Catholic emancipation
	16 November. Defeat and resignation as Prime Minister over issue of parliamentary reform
1831	**24 April.** Wife Kitty dies
1834	Becomes Chancellor of Oxford University
	Forms a 'caretaker government', then

INTRODUCTION

Arthur, Duke of Wellington is a formidable national hero; but a hero whose windows in Apsley House an enraged London mob once smashed, after failing to push over his giant 'Achilles' statue that dominated Hyde Park Corner. He was a hero who left his country no tangible inventions in an age of great inventions, not even a spinning jenny; certainly not shrapnel or rockets. Yet his memory is still brilliantly alive, and bound up with such things as a stiff upper lip, a pair of boots, a rather mysterious 'thin red line', an overwhelming victory against the dictator of Europe that he himself called 'a near run thing'. It was a victory not only for his military genius but also for his character, as expressed over a long lifetime in the spoken or written epigram – 'Nothing is worse than a battle won – except a battle lost', 'I always did the business of the day on the day.' He never put off till later what could be done today, nor lived by the Spanish word 'mañana' ('tomorrow'), though he spent so many years in Spain. Nor did he leave to others the job he himself could do better. Today he would be called a hands-on hero.

Though he was England's hero, he was not born within sound of Bow Bells, Big Ben – nor any other place in England. Ireland was his birthplace, though the exact location and exact date were long disputed. One thing can be ruled out at once. It has been claimed that Wellington said, apropos of his birth in Ireland, 'Because a man is born in a stable it does not make him a horse.' This epigram, later ascribed to him, was in fact the work of contemporary wits. It is thoroughly uncharacteristic of Wellington, both in its insult to Ireland and in its implicit claim to quasi-divine birth. His glory was very human and, as he said later of the Battle of Waterloo: 'There was glory enough for all.' He liked to remind himself and the world every so often of what is ultimately the basic fact of biography – 'I am but a man'.

Of course there are many myths and legends that fancy spins around the hero. Wellington had his share, and one new legend about him parallels a story about John Brown, who is claimed to have made his final home in American Samoa with his three daughters by Queen Victoria, driven out of Deeside by the moralists. The new legend is that Wellington seduced Queen Victoria when she was fifteen. According to this theory their son was sent to the Royal Foundling Hospital, Lisbon, and brought up as a Portuguese nobleman, though in fact he was heir to the British throne, to which, however, he never laid claim. I went to the Royal Archives to look for evidence of this bizarre story, and of course there is none whatsoever.

Wellington was a hero in his time and is a hero still. The biographer must try to find the factor in this mere man that made him different. Can the heroes of our own age give any hints?

ONE

FOOD FOR POWDER

Both the date and place of Wellington's birth were disputed. Nevertheless we must assume that Wellington himself knew best. He always celebrated it on 1 May: the year of his birth was 1769; the place, Mornington House, 6 Merrion Street (now 24 Upper Merrion Street), the Dublin home of his parents.

Lord and Lady Mornington, Wellington's father and mother, belonged to what was known in Ireland as the Protestant Ascendancy. The Morningtons' son Arthur, however, spent a childhood and youth very far removed from any kind of ascendancy. Born Arthur Wesley, the future Duke traced his descent from the Wellesleys of Somerset who first came to Ireland with Henry II in the 1170s. Gradually the Wellesleys seemed to become more Irish, acquiring a simpler family name – Wesley. But whereas Lord Mornington himself was a distinguished musician and his eldest son Richard a fine scholar, Arthur was 'food for powder and nothing more'.

That was the verdict of Arthur's own mother. Widowed in 1781 when Arthur was only twelve, anxious

1

to do her best for one daughter, Anne, and four clever sons, Richard, William, Gerald and Henry, she had no doubt that 'my awkward boy Arthur' must somehow be tipped into that universal waste-bin, the army. Unlike Richard, Arthur had not shone as a schoolboy at Eton, his chief amusement being jumping over a ditch at the bottom of his housemaster's garden. Organised games meant nothing to him. He almost certainly did not say that 'the Battle of Waterloo was won on the playing fields of Eton'. (This, in fact, was the most notorious example of epigrams being attributed to Wellington not because he was their author but because he was famous.)

As young Arthur approached manhood, his star was, if anything, even further from the ascendant. At fifteen he left Eton for life in Brighton and Brussels under tutors; then in 1786 it was Angers in France for a year at the School of Equitation. Two things that would be of utmost value to him were at last available: mastery of French and horsemanship. On Christmas Day 1787 he became a lieutenant in the 76th Regiment and two months later, an aide-de-camp to the Lord Lieutenant of Ireland. Two years after that, he was representing Trim in the Irish Parliament at Dublin.

Meanwhile, the French Revolution with all its horrors had broken out in 1789, making an indelible impression on the young Arthur. Indelible and also injurious, for henceforth Arthur was apt to equate all reform with revolution.

While climbing quietly up the military slopes, Arthur tested his worldly progress in the summer of 1793.

He proposed marriage to pretty Kitty Pakenham, daughter of Lord Longford, the Morningtons' neighbour in County Westmeath. Instructed by her brother Lord Longford (he had succeeded to the earldom), Kitty sadly refused this young army captain, who played the violin rather than playing for really high stakes as his exact contemporary Napoleon Bonaparte already did. Arthur's reaction to this blow was to tie himself up for the future. If something did occur to make Kitty or Longford change their minds, he wrote, 'my mind will still remain the same'. How could he tell? In fact he did not bother about the matter, for he was going away to the French wars and did not expect to return alive.

Within less than a year of Arthur's rejection by Kitty, Napoleon was to command all the artillery of France at Toulon. Like most young courtiers, Arthur commanded a range of debts, especially in the card-playing Dublin clubs.

In the summer of 1793 Arthur destroyed the last trace of dilettantism in his hitherto unspectacular career: he burnt his violin. Away with the young soldier-musician who read Locke's popular *Essay on Human Understanding* for pleasure. He was now a real soldier and pleased to be one. France was at war with Britain and Arthur, as of 30 September 1793, was a lieutenant-colonel who would command his brigade in Flanders for seven months from June 1794. Their commander-in-chief, 'the noble Duke of York', was a miserable failure, as was the whole campaign. Admittedly Arthur and his 33rd were withdrawn in March 1795 after a fruitless campaign in which the noble Duke of York had marched his men to the top of the hill and marched them down again.

> And when they were up they were up,
> And when they were down they were down.
> And when they were half-way up that hill
> They were neither up nor down.

But Arthur learnt much from his first campaign, disaster though it was. 'Why – I learnt what one ought not to do', he told his friend Lord Stanhope forty-five years later, 'and that is always something.' One ought not to fight General Winter without adequate food or clothing for the soldiers. One ought not to have a divided command. And at his first ever action – Boxtel in Holland – he learnt the beginnings of what one ought to do when the French charged: teach one's men to hold.

Did Arthur still feel that so far his own military career had also been neither up nor down? It seems so. On 3 May 1796 he became Colonel of the 33rd Foot and a month later he sailed with his regiment for India. The musician who had played sweetly to Kitty down by Lake Derravaragh at Pakenham Hall had indeed been banished and his place taken forever by a soldier. But a complex soldier. How often is the artist in a man extruded by the man of action? We think of the band leader suppressed in Tony Blair by the office of Prime Minister. Did the great soldier and the Prime Minister both lose something completely? Will the story of Arthur Wesley perhaps include the spiritual survival of a burnt violin?

ALL INDIA

Some people have liked to find the arbiters of their fate in a country or institution, others in a person or a book. 'Ireland caught me', said Bryan Cooper; 'Balliol bred me', wrote Hilaire Belloc. When a friend asked Wellington where all his military talents came from, he replied, 'That is all India.'

Certainly there were experiences of two wars (Mysore and 2nd Mahratta), two memorable battles, undivided military command and ability to work with the civil authorities – not so difficult considering that Arthur's dazzling brother Richard was about to become Governor-General of India. Incidentally, Arthur's family name had been changed back by Richard from the plebeian Wesley to the original Wellesley. No doubt these extra three letters helped to add authenticity to the family's place in the aristocracy.

In attributing his basic military success to India, Wellington would add one vital personal quality to the honest catalogue of assets revealed to Stanhope: 'The real reason why I succeeded in my own campaigns', he concluded, 'is because I was always on the spot – I saw everything and did everything for myself.' This trait was to emerge and develop in India, until Arthur

Wellesley found himself saying roundly: 'I like to walk alone.'

Meanwhile, British imperial power in India was threatened from within as well as by the French outside. And as the jewel in the imperial crown, India had to be defended. The noble beast that Wellesley had to tame was Tippoo, the Tiger of Mysore. Though still sending 'happy letters' to the English, Tippoo Sultan was in league with the French. Mysore was to be invaded by Arthur Wellesley on Richard's orders of 3 February 1799. 'I wish to God the whole [expedition] were under your direction', continued Richard, 'but even as it is [with General Harris in overall command] I think our success is certain. . . .' Arthur's second-in-command was not so certain. Major-General David Baird, Wellesley's senior by twelve years and imprisoned for over three years by Tippoo, was sadly jealous. He had wanted to head the force against Tippoo. Arthur, however, had valuable Indian Allies in the Nizam of Hyderabad and his sepoys.

Seringapatam, Tippoo's capital, was surrounded by 'topes' (thickets) and the assault could not begin until the bamboo, betel and cocoa had been thoroughly cleared. Assigning himself the dangerous task of scouring the exceptionally deep Sultanpettah tope, Arthur incurred one of the few personal failures of his career on 5 April 1799: he got lost in the heat and darkness and was eventually found dead asleep with his head on the messroom table. From this minor disaster, Arthur drew another major 'what not to do' to guide his future: night operations should not be undertaken unless absolutely unavoidable.

Next day, 6 April, the Sultanpettah tope was finally cleared and on 4 May the assault was ordered. The storming party was led by Baird – at his own wish – and Tippoo fell at the North Gate, not skulking in the palace as the 33rd had expected. Today the jewelled Uma bird from his turban is at Windsor while the famous mechanical tiger from Mysore can be seen in the Victoria & Albert Museum, its tigerish growl grown pathetically asthmatic. Prize money was divided among the 'haves' with the usual eye to justice à la eighteenth century: £150,000 to General Harris, £4,000 to Lieutenant-Colonel Wellesley, £5 each to the Indian surgeons and sepoys. Arthur was still insolvent, that is if Richard cared to call in his debts.

After some manoeuvring with Baird, Arthur was confirmed in command. He left Mysore and the south for the Deccan where he ran to ground a notorious bandit, who styled himself the king of earth and heaven; in fact, he commanded an army, and was the bearer of the interesting name Dhoondiah Waugh. Waugh and 5,000 cavalry were rounded up on 10 September 1800, and the king of earth and heaven killed. With King Waugh safely despatched to heaven, Colonel Wellesley and his army moved northwards.

After both the Battle of Boxtel and the Battle of Seringapatam Wellington showed interest in the development of his new military tactic: persuading steady troops to stand their ground without firing while the enemy approached; then when the enemy was really close, to drive him off with rolling volleys of musketry.

Wellesley then marched north for what was to be the second Mahratta War. He was to conduct a successful siege and fight two famous battles, Assaye being among the greatest of his career.

At the same time, the Wellesley family were going up and up – Richard a marquess (1799), Arthur a major-general (1802) and two other brothers rising in the church. And great events had shaken the world beyond. Ireland's parliament, in which Arthur Wellesley had sat, was swept away after the '98 Rebellion and Ireland was forced into union with England by the Act of Union of Great Britain and Ireland (1800). For just over a year there was peace with Bonaparte's France (Peace of Amiens, March 1802–May 1803) and the street rhymesters celebrated the replacement of William Pitt the greatest of war leaders by the unmemorable Henry Addington:

> Pitt is to Addington
> As London is to Paddington.

The Napoleonic War was renewed with Pitt again Prime Minister just as Colonel Wellesley was preparing India for the renewal of war with the Mahrattas (May and August 1803). This was Arthur's first great chance to test his powers against an enemy that was attacking its neighbours. News reached him that the Mahratta Governor of Poona planned to burn it down before evacuating. He intended to restore the Peshwah to the city, but to restore him to a smoking ruin would have

been a fatal blow to prestige. So Wellesley, with 400
cavalry, covered forty miles by night and when he
dashed into Poona on 20 April 1803 the city was in
turmoil but untouched.

War was declared against Scindiah, the Mahratta
chief, on 6 August. First came the siege and capture of
Ahmednuggur, Scindiah's mighty fortress. The siege
involved Major-General Wellesley in bringing his army
across rivers by fords or in basket-boats in the manner of
Alexander the Great. The garrison surrendered on 12
August. Wellington's favourite memory of the siege
centred on a young soldier falling from the top rung of a
scaling ladder, picking himself up and re-entering the
fray. He was Colin Campbell, Wellington's future private
secretary and Governor of Ceylon. Wellington liked to
joke that he had first seen this grand Sir Colin 'in the
air'.

The village of Assaye, standing on a wide shimmering
plain with the River Kaitna in front and green parrots
and kites above, was the unlikely site of Wellesley's most
challenging Indian battle. Outnumbered seven to one by
Scindiah's French-trained cavalry, infantry and artillery,
the small British force at first appeared to be hopelessly
cut off from its objective. There was no ford across the
Kaitna, declared Wellesley's guide. But one of
Wellesley's already dominant characteristics took over in
the crisis: the urge to see everything for himself. A long
look through his glass soon convinced him that there
could not be two villages facing each other across the
Kaitna, and just downstream from Assaye, without there

being some means of communication between them. He found the ford.

Years later Wellington added a typical comment to an account of the operation: if 'one is strongly intent on an object, *common sense* will usually direct one to the right means'. Assaye was a bloody battle. After much brilliant manoevring by both sides, when each tried to exploit the waters of the Kaitna or its tributary the Juah and the land between, Wellesley ordered the assault. Assaye was a murderous affair that left Wellesley wrapped in gloom. He was to feel the same melancholy after Waterloo, another 'near-run thing', though that memorable phrase had not yet come to him. When he finally slept after the victory, a nightmare visited him: every single soldier had been killed. In fact the victors lost nearly 1,600 killed or wounded to their enemy's 6,000. Every single one of Wellesley's staff lost a horse, Colin Campbell three and Wellesley two. There was heroic courage displayed on both sides, by Scindiah's Mahrattas, and by Wellesley's sepoys, and Europeans, including Germans. Years later, when the trees that Wellington had stood under at Assaye and Waterloo, a mango and an elm, had both died of their wounds and been made into boxes and chairs, he was asked what was the best thing in the way of fighting he ever did: 'Assaye', he answered glumly and said not another word. As a direct result of Assaye, Wellesley had deeper and more humane things to say on the balance between victory, defeat or retreat. Less than three weeks after the battle he was writing his official despatch: 'I should

not like to see again such loss as I sustained on the
23 September [Assaye], even if attended by such a gain.'
Assaye was a black diamond in Arthur's Indian crown –
dazzling but deathly. He went on to win and win, but
without the intense horrors.

Subsequently, the Mahratta stronghold of Argaum
was captured and Gawilghur surrendered. It was before
Argaum that another Indian pearl was added to the
Wellesley legend. Seeing a cloud of dust on the horizon
Arthur realised it must be Colonel Stevenson and his
forces who had lost their way and so had missed Assaye.
A delighted Indian on Arthur's staff realised that his
wonderful general could now distinguish one kind of
Indian dust from another! Wellesley also personally reformed a panicking remnant of the Assaye heroes before
Argaum. The men of the advance-guard, alarmed by the
Mahrattas' artillery onslaught and disconcerted by
the great sea of high corn before them obscuring their
view, wanted to turn and run. Wellesley first waved his
sword and shouted in a vain attempt to persuade them
to stand their ground but at last he gave up, sent them to
the rear and then brought them forward again, under
cover of his own guns. Commenting frankly afterwards,
he said: 'If I had not been there to restore the battle, we
should have lost the day.'

Twenty-one years after Sir Arthur Wellesley completed
his Indian mission, the Indian writer J.R. Teejeebhoy
was still thanking him on behalf of the Indian people.
However, it is probable that the surrender of Gawilghur,
an almost impregnable Mahratta fortress, north-east of

Argaum, on 15 December 1803 had never required an all-out assault by Wellesley's relatively slender force. The brilliant American military historian, the late Jac Weller, personally examined the sites of all Wellington's battles and sieges in 1968. He told the present writer that three determined troops of boy scouts armed with rocks could have repulsed several times their number. The assumption is that Arthur Wellesley's awe-inspiring reputation for invincible military power had already marched ahead of him from Ahmednuggur and Assaye, convincing the Mahrattas of Gawilghur that surrender was the better part of valour.

Arthur Wellesley had been created a Knight of Bath on 1 September 1804. There was perhaps a hidden irony in the timing of the honour, for he was taking powerful medicinal baths to cure a painful skin infection: his bathwater scorched the towels. Indeed, Arthur Wellesley's general health was deteriorating: lumbago, rheumatism, fevers – all were on the increase. He had negotiated peace with Scindiah but powerful Mahrattas like Holkar were still a problem. Wellesley had been eight years in India. He had a burning urge for home. He wanted no more tombstones on India's coast, such as the writer William Hickey had described:

> Mynheer Gludenstack lies here,
> Who intended to go home last year.

The name Arthur Wellesley would fit the rhythm just as well as poor Mynheer Gludenstack.

1804 was Arthur's last full year in India. He embarked for home on 10 March 1805 and landed at Dover in September, after calling in at the very pleasant island of St Helena. Napoleon had been crowned Emperor in 1804. By 1804 Arthur was not quite a nabob but he was worth £50,000. At any rate, they were a very good match.

THREE

THE BRIDGE
YEARS, 1806–9

Wellington's life work was not to begin until 1809, with the Peninsular War proper and his own acclaimed leadership. But the years that bridged his return from India and his departure for Portugal were of immense importance to him, militarily, politically, emotionally. It is sad and ironic to think that the bullet which killed the great Sir John Moore at Corunna in January 1809 was a silver bullet for Wellington, because it was after Corunna that Arthur moved right to the top.

His newly acquired reputation in India for flirtation with married ladies was not to prove an obstacle, for he was saved at this stage by the woman who had turned him down in 1793 – Kitty Pakenham. Kitty had never married and had become pathetically pale and worn in the long barren years between Arthur's departure and return. Of course Arthur also was still unmarried, which perhaps gave Mrs Olivia Sparrow, Kitty's best friend, the idea of acting as an intermediary and persuading Arthur that Kitty was waiting for him. As a man of honour he must try again. But was he a man of honour? He had certainly fallen in love with a dark-haired beauty in India,

Mrs John Freese, but there is no evidence that he was the natural father of her son, his godson Arthur Freese. Indeed, a painting of young Freese at Stratfield Saye shows him with his legal father's typical sandy hair. The truth is that the destruction of Arthur Wellesley's violin had left a gap to be filled in youth by pretty women and romantic fiction. His book-box on the boat home contained such volumes as *Love at First Sight* and *Lessons for Lovers*. One lesson that he missed was that endless waiting does not improve young women.

He proposed to Kitty and was accepted. When he entered the Longfords' Dublin drawing-room with his brother for the wedding ceremony on 10 April 1806 he was struck dumb – or rather, not quite dumb enough. 'She has grown ugly, by Jove!', he whispered to Gerald. All the bright colour had faded. But then they had neither met nor written for at least eleven years. Nevertheless, within less than two years Kitty had given him two sons, Arthur and Charles, his heirs. The marriage was not a success but it endured – just. Arthur wrote Kitty rude notes when she spent her household money on dubious charities. She felt herself inadequate and he made her feel a fool. But eventually she was to prove herself worthy by helping other inadequate people. Why did he marry her? It was he who was the fool, he later confessed. He did it without thought, expecting to fall on some battlefield anyway. There was a vein of despondent fatalism in the man who had renounced the support of his violin; a vein that had to be dealt with by other means.

Politics and the army were interwoven in Wellesley's life for the three years after his return home. Back in England on 10 September 1805, he found himself only two days later waiting in the Colonial Office in Downing Street to see Lord Castlereagh, the minister. There was another person waiting. Wellesley immediately recognised the gentleman with one arm, but Nelson, of course, did not recognise the crop-haired and deeply sunburnt sepoy general. He talked rather too much. Then he realised, as Arthur later put it, 'that I was somebody' and found out who. Nelson immediately changed his tune, and conversed charmingly as with an equal. History was in fact staging one of its most attractive tableaux. Nelson would leave Downing Street to fight Trafalgar only six weeks later, while Wellesley's Peninsular prologue was less than three years off. Moreover, the meeting with Nelson probably did its work in humbling young Arthur. Returning home from India after being fêted as a mixture of nabob and an Indian prince, Arthur Wellesley now found himself just 'somebody'.

However, Wellesley was soon to find himself again somebody special. The dying William Pitt rode very slowly from Wimbledon Common to London, while young Arthur again expounded Richard's 'Indian system' of Mahratta alliances to the apparently open-minded Prime Minister. More importantly, Arthur heard Pitt's memorable two-minute speech on the war in Europe – his last: 'England saved herself [from Napoleon] by her exertions, and will, as I trust, save Europe by her example.' Pitt's tremendous words struck home to Arthur, who had always felt himself the 'retained servant' of king and country. He would need heartening over the next few months, for Bonaparte's defeat of Austria and Russia at Austerlitz (December 1805) meant that Arthur Wellesley and the brigade he had just taken to the Elbe had to be brought home without firing a shot. Posted to Hastings, he became MP for Rye, next door in east Sussex. This was followed by a seat in Cornwall and then by one at Newport on the Isle of Wight. It was easy in the unreformed Parliament of the early nineteenth century to pop Sir Arthur Wellesley into a safe Tory seat with which he had no personal connection but made it his business to use as a means of defending in the House of Commons Richard's Indian record. When Portland's Tory ministry was formed in April 1807, Arthur became Irish Chief Secretary.

Arthur regarded his new job as definitely outside the war in Europe. As such it did not satisfy him. 'It was an Irish potato tho' a gilt potato', his salary being £6,566 a year, no less. So when the government organised a secret expedition to Europe, he leapt at the command. His 'dearest' but excitable Kitty was not told until almost the moment of sailing, 31 July 1807. Wellesley was the choice of George Canning, an exceptionally strong Foreign Secretary determined to resist Bonaparte's latest war plan: a system to starve out Britain by blockading it. Neutrals were to be invited – in other words forced – to assist the blockade by surrendering their fleets, if they had any, to the Emperor of the French.

Denmark was a neutral and too uncomfortably close to England for Canning to risk seeing its fine fleet in French hands. Invited to hand over their ships to England instead, the Danes firmly refused. But the Danish militiamen could not be expected to outfight picked British regulars. They were overpowered – though only, in the end, thanks to Wellington's crucial part in the operation. It was his brigade that effected the first landings, set about investing Copenhagen and cut off possible reinforcements. The expedition created a minimum of bitterness. Wellesley got the garrison to surrender without a regular bombardment of their lovely city. He had already fought side by side with one of his two superiors. Sir David Baird, of old Madras days, commanded a division. The other, 'a steady old guardsman', Sir Harry Burrard, was second-in-command to General Cathcart's overall control. Wellesley was to see much of both Burrard and Baird in the Peninsula – not all of it pleasant. As is so often said of politics, so too of the armed forces: 'there is no friendship at the top'.

After Copenhagen the Lord-Lieutenant of Ireland clawed back his Chief Secretary, but at least this brief action had brought forward his name in Europe. Better still, it was a good name. One of his Danish opponents thanked him for his 'humane and generous conduct'. When a rebellion against Bonaparte broke out in Spain and Portugal in 1808, Arthur Wellesley was put in temporary command of an expeditionary force sent to the people's aid.

For the first time he was commanding an army that did not think their Major-General was prematurely bald; his close attention to hygiene had led him to favour cropped hair over pigtails or powder. In the army of 1807–8 he was not alone in this: under new regulations powder and pigtails were out. In Arthur's book-box this time was a Spanish prayer-book, presented to him by his friends, the two Ladies of Langollen, famous for their romantic friendship.

Before leaving England, Arthur had invited the writer John Wilson Croker to dinner at his home at 11 Harley Street. After Kitty had retired, Arthur gave Croker a brief but inspired view of his future against the French: 'My die is cast, they may overwhelm me, but I don't think they will out-manoeuvre me.' It was Wellesley's genius for manoeuvre that saved him from being 'more than half-beaten before the battle was begun' – like the Continental armies of Ulm and Austerlitz. 'I, at least, will not be frightened beforehand.'

Wellesley began his landings in Mondego Bay, Portugal, on 30 July 1808. But the news from the Foreign Office was bad. A letter marked 'secret' revealed that the French army in Portugal under General Junot was too strong to be tackled by Wellesley and his 9,000. He was to be reinforced with 15,000 men and superseded in command by Sir Hew Dalrymple, aged sixty, with Sir Harry Burrard as second-in-command, just as he had been at Copenhagen. And Arthur? Back at the bottom again.

Despite the way that Arthur Wellesley's so far thwarted history seemed to be repeating itself, he was about to begin one of the most remarkable wars of the century. And the utter inadequacy of those put over him – old Sir Hew and Sir Harry – finally was to make his own command inevitable. Perhaps, if Sir John Moore had not died and Sir David Baird had not lost an arm, Sir Arthur Wellesley would have returned yet again to No. 3. But that is war.

Arthur's troops began landing on 1 August. After a preliminary action at Obidos, he set about the capture of Roliça, the first important village on the high road to Lisbon – and the first battle of the Peninsular War, which was to last until 1814. Unfortunately Roliça was not an engagement that offered Wellesley the chance to display his new tactics. In any case Napoleon Bonaparte failed to recognise anything special about Arthur Wellesley. Not so the French generals.

Roliça began at dawn on 17 August 1808 with disaster and finished in desperate victory. Thanks to a premature dash up a steep gully behind the French lines by Colonel Lake's 29th Foot which resulted in his force being cut off, most of his men captured and himself killed, Wellesley ordered an immediate advance in the face of preliminary disaster, and his total force of British skirmishers followed by infantry compelled the French to retreat, losing three guns. Roliça might have been a desperate defeat; Wellesley called it a desperate victory – not the new way to drive the French out of the Peninsula. The Battle of Vimeiro was to be more like it, though Napoleon still noticed nothing new. After all, Wellesley was only an Anglo-Irish general who had commanded British armies in India – a sepoy general. (The term sepoy when connected with a white man in those days, made him not quite the thing.)

On the morning after Roliça, Wellesley heard that the 4,000 reinforcements he had dreaded, plus their commander Sir Harry Burrard, were about to land. By 20 August Sir Hew was ready to supersede him. Wellesley was then in the hills above Vimeiro, a village nearer to Lisbon than Roliça by quite a few miles. Wellesley proposed to outflank the French and capture royal Mafra above Lisbon. Burrard said wait – for yet more reinforcements. The very next day Andoche Junot, the French general in Portugal, gave Wellesley his chance, Burrard or no Burrard.

Junot moved his men westwards to surprise the much smaller British army. Wellesley acted immediately with the radical deployment of his whole force, the bulk of his army hidden as far as possible from sight of the enemy and the rest on a parallel green hump with a flat top – Vimeiro Hill. Meanwhile, the French advanced in Napoleon's traditional order: a magical mixture, as it always turned out, of swarming skirmishers in front of invincible infantry. This time, however, it was the new Wellesley magic that worked. As the French went in, column after column, they were met by rifle fire and a twelve-gun cannonade. It was no deterrent. The French expected it. Suddenly Wellesley's infantry, who had been ordered to lie down behind the crest of Vimeiro Hill and hold their fire till the last moment, found the last moment had come. So did the French attackers – but in another sense. A 'thin red line' of scarlet-uniformed British infantry ('thin' because it was only two soldiers deep, so that every man could fire, whereas the French were in a dense, self-destroying oblong sixty men deep) seemed to rise from nowhere and open a rolling fire into the helpless French target. The hapless French were tightly packed into such a solid rectangle thirty feet broad and forty-two feet deep that they were unable to deploy. Their leaders relentlessly enveloped, they faltered; they retreated; they broke and fled.

In the streets of Vimeiro Wellesley saw British cavalry go out of control – not for the last time. But after the western ridge was similarly cleared, Vimeiro was a victory, no doubt. And Wellesley called on Sir Harry to go for Lisbon. Wellesley would be there in three days. The tired old man's mind was still on reinforcements. 'No', he said, 'wait for Moore.' It was not a bad pun, though it was a bad mistake. Bonaparte needed to see the French driven into the sea in order to revise his ideas of the British army. Instead of which he was to see General Junot making a most astute advantageous peace in place of deteriorating war.

It was called the Convention of Cintra, for it was in the beautiful town of Cintra that it was drawn up. The terms, as devised by the clever French General Kellerman, envisaged all the Portuguese fortresses flying royal standards once more (made from royal sheets cut down to size) and the French . . . well, the beaten French would be free to sail away, not a jot the worse. Wellesley was ordered to sign the Convention. He obeyed without even reading the text, most reluctantly. Why did he not refuse? The answer is two-fold. First, he agreed with the armistice in principle, though not in detail. Second, actual good nature. This is the kind of complexity that makes a person human. In Arthur it was his good nature that vied with his vein of iron. He was both to be an 'Iron Duke' and a 'Namuk-wallah' (Indian for a loyal servant). They went well together. London read the Convention on 31 September and raged against it. The poet Byron spoke for all in his *Childe Harold*: 'Britain sickens, Cintra! at thy name.' Arthur, too, said he was sick of it all.

Three major-generals – Sir Hew, Sir Harry and Sir Arthur – were recalled to a judicial court of inquiry sitting in Chelsea Great Hall; and though none of the three was sentenced, Sir Hew and Sir Harry never held command again, while Sir Arthur was glad to get back to his civilian post in Ireland. It was the Portuguese people who were to upset Kellerman's apple-cart.

Meanwhile, nothing was too bad for the Wellesleys. Richard was still under attack for his Indian policy and his main attacker, James Paull, had just blown his own brains out because of gambling debts. Somehow it seemed to be the Wellesleys' fault. Henry had just been deserted by his wife, the mother of his four young children, who had eloped in a hackney coach with a cavalry officer, the future Marquess of Anglesey.

And yet here was Arthur by April 1809 calling himself the 'Child of Fortune'.

FORTRESS PORTUGAL

A s so often in Arthur Wellesley's life, what had seemed bad news was quickly changed into good. So infuriated was the Emperor Napoleon by the thought of the British descent on Portugal that he set about driving out this 'hideous leopard' himself. His new insult for the English was, of course, taken from the heraldic leopards on the royal standard.

The latest French attack culminated in a shattering blow for Britain. At Corunna General Sir David Baird lost an arm, General Sir Harry Burrard a son, and General Sir John Moore his life. This last was the end of a reforming genius in the British army. Though Moore was a Whig, Tory Arthur Wellesley had met him in Portugal and liked him. It was he who inspired Arthur with the valuable thought that the party system – Whigs against Tories – must not prevent the army from getting the best men. Who were the winning generals to take Moore's place? There was Wellesley . . . and Wellesley . . . and Wellesley.

Sir John Moore had fallen on 16 January 1809. By 12 April, Sir Arthur Wellesley was on the high seas, taking a force to defend Portugal. He had resigned his Irish Chief Secretaryship and had assured the government that Portugal could be defended on certain terms: 20,000 British troops and 4,000 cavalry; a reconstituted Portuguese army; and the Spaniards to pin down as many French troops as possible. Forget Spain, replied Wellesley's government, and clear Portugal.

Never did Wellesley regret the following challenging sentence in his memorandum of 7 March 1809 to the War Minister Lord Castlereagh: 'I have always been of the opinion that Portugal might be defended.' Never, except perhaps for a moment on 12 April when General Sir Arthur Wellesley suddenly heard that 'the end is near'. These were the words of the captain of the ship transporting him to Portugal. A sudden violent storm had caused the man to send for Arthur to come up on deck wearing his boots. Arthur replied that he could swim better without his boots and would stay where he was. The weather adjusted itself to match Arthur's calm. And Portugal would be defended after all.

A secret crossing of the great River Douro by night in wine barges opened the assault of 12 May on the celebrated city of Oporto. As a growing force of redcoats scrambled up the steep northern bank of the river, a corresponding stream of French fugitives lost itself in the wild country beyond the city. Caught unawares, Marshal Soult and his army escaped across the wilderness, jettisoning guns and baggage, and occasionally hanging a Portuguese peasant – a grisly sight that hardened Wellesley's resolve to pursue the chase.

Oporto was liberated; the French were run out of the country in five days; Portugal was freed. General Wellesley had thrown a web of magic over Oporto, calling it his greatest adventure, but his philosophy was to make a dash against the enemy only when it was safe to do so. He was a 'safe' general, said his colleague General William Beresford, not a 'cautious' one.

Perhaps the secret advances by water and moonlight in Oporto justified his enthusiasm, but the next thrill – Talavera – was to be more sombre. This, the next spectacular action of the Peninsular War, was to be fought in Spain. By the conclusion of the episode in 1812, Arthur Wellesley's extraordinary genius was becoming clear.

A couplet from Byron's *Childe Harold* epic gave the first hint of something ominous at Talavera:

> Three hosts combine to offer sacrifice
> To feed the crow on Talavera's plain.

One might well imagine that Macbeth's three witches joined with the three hosts in superintending their sacrifice. The French were led by a General Victor – surely nothing ominous about that – while the ancient Spanish commander, Cuesta, required four sturdy Sancho Panzas to hoist him onto his stallion and to lift him down again. In fact the Spanish host combined with the British under Wellesley's leadership, their numbers reaching 55,000 against the French 22,000.

As for the commander of the third host on the battlefield, Sir Arthur Wellesley narrowly avoided offering the supreme sacrifice before the fighting at Talavera had begun. While he was making his usual personal investigations of local topographical features from the top of the Casa da Salinas' twin towers, a French force clattered into the courtyard – but not quite in time to prevent General Wellesley and his staff from dashing down the stone steps and away with an even greater roar and rattle. It was a blessing for his army that Wellesley escaped, for the force was a plundering rabble that could not handle success.

Wellesley crossed the Spanish border on 4 July 1809. Through the city of Talavera ran the road to Madrid if you travelled east and to the west, the route back to Portugal. The battlefield was on the plain. Its features included the Portina stream running north–south through a gulley and cutting the area in two. Above all, in every sense, was the high fort of the Medellin, standing guard over the northern mountains. It was here that the chilling excitement of the battle began.

In the creepy darkness of 27 July a British force of 20,000, under popular General Sir Rowland 'Daddy' Hill, surprised the French, who had failed to post pickets, and toppled them out of the Medellin. After the agony was over – 300 dead men on each side – Wellesley slept a few hours in his famous blue battle cape. It was a red dawn. Against the warning sky the 'victors' of the Medellin could see the black mass of a huge French army 40,000 strong, gathered to block Wellesley's way into Spain. At Talavera a civilised thread was woven into the barbarous pattern of war. A truce was called during the violent early heat of 28 July and both sides washed and drank in the Portina, until the French drums beat the recall, nods and smiles vanished, and the hands that had shaken each other returned to the trigger. Wellesley himself encouraged the French custom of giving notice of advance to save the life of the odd scout. Did these practices demonstrate the horrible artificiality of war? Or the necessary inclusiveness of war in humanity's tapestry?

After three powerful French attacks on the 28th, a fourth assault from the rear plunged the Anglo-Spanish army into so severe a crisis that Wellesley himself personally organised the rescue. The remnants of one Guards brigade and two brigades of the King's German Legion had dashed across the Portina in excitement and into the unbroken French columns beyond. Of the Guards' 2,000 men, 600 fell and the hole they left in their own front was about to be filled with French cavalry and guns. The fate of the day depended on how Wellesley handled the crisis. Somehow he managed to gather 3,000 men and into the hole in the front marched the 48th led by Hill, opening their ranks for a moment to let the Guards retreat then closing the line again: the French were held. With their spirits flagging, the French attacks diminished; by morning they had vanished, knowing that Marshal Soult and his thousands were marching towards Portugal.

The doleful Kitty was ecstatic when the news reached England in mid-August. As for the British government, Talavera was – had to be – a victory, and to seal and celebrate it, they gave Arthur his overdue peerage. On 4 September 1809 he was gazetted Viscount Wellington of Talavera and Wellington (a town in Somerset near the Wellesleys' original home). A Portuguese engraver decorated Lord Wellington's portrait with the added title, 'Invicto', to which Arthur replied: 'Don't halloo till you are out of the wood.'

Meanwhile, the once green grass on the crest of the Medellin had been burnt black by the French fire, scorching the wounded and roasting the dead horses. It was the most 'Murderous Battle' he had ever known. Wellington would halloo, but not till the French were out of Spain.

Suddenly all the news was bad again. Instead of hearing that the French were quitting Spain the Spanish commander Cuesta learnt that they were advancing on Talavera with strong reinforcements. Wellington felt it necessary to retreat into Portugal once more to make sure of its defence. Cuesta promised to care for the wounded of Talavera, but the moment the British had gone, Cuesta followed, leaving the wounded to the advancing French. Wellington took the news badly, not because he expected French atrocities – he knew they would treat his wounded well. It was, as he said, the shame. . . .

Wellington also had trouble back in Britain to contend with. Much of the press refused to accept that Talavera was, or ever had been, a victory. And the government had its own difficulties. Two Cabinet ministers, Castlereagh and Canning, fought a duel, partly because the latter tried to lay the blame for the retreat at Talavera on the former. It was Wellington's task to persuade everybody that while retreat from Talavera was essential, retreat from Portugal would be fatal.

As his army withdrew once again, it too had its shames and disgraces. The camp-followers, loaded with plunder, were duly given the lash after being caught red-handed in cellars when too drunk to escape British military justice, or often drowned in the flooded cellars before the dreaded lash could torture them. Wellington should have exempted the women? But they were (of necessity) the worse plunderers. And the British army lived by friendly civilian relationships – paying for all it used, instead of extracting food from the civil population by force as the French did.

At last Wellington and his chief engineer rode into a hilly quadrilateral of Portugal that was to witness the most creative drama of the whole Peninsular War. It was also to be one of Wellington's most imaginative contributions to military history and was summed up in the following words carved on a Portuguese monument: 'They shall not pass'. The Lines of Torres Vedras created by Wellington and his chief engineer were a beautifully subtle defence system and also a closely guarded military secret.

The quadrangle that contained the Lines was locked in by Torres Vedras itself in the north, Lisbon in the south, the River Tagus in the east and the Atlantic Ocean to the west. The idea for the defences was evolved by Wellington in his usual way: out of his own head, with the supporting advice of professionals. He summed up this method in characteristic words: 'I will get up my Horse and take a look; and then tell you!' This time his 'look' was to take him and his engineers several weeks to complete; then the Lines had to be constructed from the 'look'. But at last they were ready for the army to enter. Today if you are lucky enough to know a kindly Portuguese engineer he may show you the elaborate pattern of defences – the surviving stone walls, the charming roof gardens that are really covering gun emplacements, the endless short trenches and earthworks, sloping at last to a flat green shore sprinkled with perfectly peaceful butterflies. The mountain ranges were used to draw the actual 'Lines'.

By September 1810 the mysterious defensive Lines of Torres Vedras were quite ready to receive Wellington's army – 51,000 men altogether, half British, half what Wellington called his Portuguese fighting cocks. But before they could make their final retreat for the winter, the Allied forces had to fight off a powerful army of 65,000 Frenchmen about to assault the great Bussaco hogsback (nearly ten miles long) on which the Allies were stationed.

On 27 September 1810 was fought one of the definitive battles of the Peninsular War. At about 6 a.m. 14,000 Frenchmen burst upwards through autumn mists.

Today you can still see the cart-track they used among the wild rocks and trees, until it meets a new forestry road and disappears. The village of San Antonia is still at the bottom, the windmill of Sula at the top and Wellington's headquarters, the Convent of Bussaco, still crowns the ridge, but is now a hotel. Wellington again had recourse to the novel tactics he had invented in India and then worked out in the Peninsula at Roliça and Vimeiro. He allowed the active, speedy French to rush almost to the summit of Bussaco ridge, keeping his well-trained, highly disciplined troops concealed behind the crest. Then suddenly the moment came. At a signal, the Allied ranks sprang up and drove the French down again, their bayonets sparkling, as the historian Napier declared, like a deadly waterfall. By nightfall the fighting was over and the Allies were left to make their way into the town of Torres Vedras (the old towers), from which the first Line of Torres Vedras started, entering them from 8 October 1810. They moved in through deep autumn and winter fogs, so that every post became a listening post.

No attempts by the French to capture the Lines were to succeed, for Wellington had persuaded the patriotic Portuguese to adopt a scorched earth policy. Thus their usual method of living off the land in every enemy country was thwarted. There was no food to be requisitioned and in the early months of 1811 the French were obliged to retreat into the two great border fortresses of Ciudad Rodrigo and Badajoz.

Portugal had been defended, as Wellington said it could and would be, given the troops and money to pay for their supplies. Forgotten were the press and the parliamentary Opposition, which had demanded the evacuation of the Peninsula. And if there were sometimes little difficulties with Portugal itself, why, Wellington could deal with them too. One British party sent out to buy food was ordered to bow to the landlords. Of course they could not possibly do that. They returned proud but empty-handed. So Wellington set out instead, returning later well loaded with supplies. 'How did you do it?', asked his staff in amazement. 'Oh I just bobbed down. . . .' Britain's latest hero was cast in a new mould: unshakeable self-confidence balanced by an ordinary man's approach to life. In the world of trees he would have been a pliant willow, not a brittle elm.

The situation was sorry on both sides when the fogs of spring began. The French besieging army under Marshal Massena had dwindled to 40,000 men and the all-important woman, Madame X (Massena's notorious mistress, who had to have her luxuries smuggled through the English lines). Wellington's army was improving, but it still plundered and he still demanded better recruits.

Suddenly everything changed again. On 5 March Massena decamped. At last the besiegers were the pursued and the 'Hideous English Leopard' was again rampant.

FIVE

INTO SPAIN

There was to be a new Wellington and a new war. Even the Whigs praised him. He must exchange his economy and caution for a spirit of advance. And he was trusted by his men. As John Kincaid of the Rifles wrote: 'We would rather see his long nose in a fight than a reinforcement of ten thousand men any day.' The war, he had predicted, would take on a 'new shape' – it would become offensive.

In order to unlock Spain it was necessary to capture its two border fortresses, Ciudad Rodrigo in the north and Badajoz to the south. They were the keys of Spain. As spring turned to summer, both sides tried manoeuvring. There were some minor but bloody actions, and the appalling carnage at Albuera on 16 May 1811 when Beresford was in charge and Wellington up in the north. At one point a French prisoner reported to Wellington that the whole French army was in his front. 'Oh, they are all there, are they?', said the imperturbable general. 'Well, we must mind a little what we are about.'

By June the time was ripe for Wellington to lay siege to Badajoz. He wrote sombrely on 8 June: 'Badajoz may fall . . . but the business will be very near run on both sides.' (His friends were to hear those words again four years later – after Waterloo.) After two failed British assaults on the town news came that 60,000 French were closing in on Badajoz and Wellington had to withdraw. The army's worst enemy now – mid-June – was dysentery, known as King Agrippa.

Marshal Massena was the only one of Napoleon's commanders who had kept Wellington awake at night. He was now replaced by Marshal Marmont. Despite everything, Wellington still felt he should try to stay on the offensive and he blockaded Ciudad Rodrigo that August. However, it was relieved by Marmont and for three cold months, October to December, the Allies recuperated in winter quarters. In January 1812 a great attack on Ciudad Rodrigo was in preparation. The Allies dared not wait longer, for Marmont was again far away, at Salamanca. On 8 January, the heroic Colonel Colborne and his volunteers seized the main outworks and by the 19th Wellington was writing out the order of attack for that night, guns firing all around.

Ciudad Rodrigo was (and is) a delightful fortress, with a Roman bridge over the River Agueda. Fortunately in 1812 the governor and troops manning the fortress were unable to resist the Allied assaults on the breaches. Ciudad Rodrigo fell – but according to the rules of war, such as they were, the town could not be pillaged, because its garrison had surrendered. In fact, as ever, there were crazy drunks among General Picton's 3rd Foot who required his huge Welsh voice to call them off from the plundering and parts of the town were indeed sacked. But there was nothing to compare with the horrors of Badajoz.

Badajoz, the second key to Spain, looked grim and displayed a mood of black hostility. Wellington had never seen such thick, battered walls before and as the dead began to lie thick in the breaches, he wept. The story of the siege was one of constant horrors and heroism relieved by a rare joke or romance. The strong defiant town was mercilessly sacked and put to the sword, but a lovely Spanish girl of fourteen was rescued from the massacre by one of Wellington's dashing officers, Harry Smith. In due course they married. Later still, Sir Harry was to call a famous South African town Ladysmith after his wife. Others were not so lucky, and there was the familiar soldiers' joke about 'Ben Battle who left his legs in Badajoz breaches'. The fortress was entered on 7 April 1812 amid pandemonium.

With the keys to Spain safely in his pocket, Wellington was ready to go on the full offensive by summer 1812. Was the advance to start from Badajoz so that he could throw Marshal Soult out of southern Spain? Or from Ciudad Rodrigo, to drive Marmont from Salamanca and the centre?

Marmont had returned to the celebrated university city after his recent failures and it would resound mightily to Wellington's credit if he could force the Marshal back yet again. So on 13 June 1812, 43,000 British and Portuguese plus 3,000 Spaniards crossed the River Aqueda at Ciudad Rodrigo and marched eastwards, towards Salamanca, the Pyrenees – and

France. On the way, a trivial incident testified to Wellington's unique image with the army. Lieutenant Arthur Shakespeare recalled: 'I saw the Duke of Wellington quietly pull his boot off and scratch his foot.' One feels there ought to have been a clap of thunder at least to mark this godlike act. The Duke's officers had taken to calling him 'the Beau' or 'the Peer', especially his admiring fellow officer and brother-in-law Ned Pakenham, who also referred to Arthur as 'the Man of Energy', while the Spanish thought of his nose, and shouted 'The Eagle! The Eagle!'. He got quite used to being kissed by Spanish women.

Salamanca turned out to be Ned Pakenham's finest hour. The battle to hold it and expand the British grip eastwards was fought on 22 July 1812. It began as a strange parallel march by the two hostile armies along an extensive valley, with the French slightly ahead. Then they suddenly came upon two little flat-topped hills, the Arapiles, of which Marmont promptly seized the greater, and then boldly extended his left to cut off the Allied leaders, despising them as brave soldiers who could not manoeuvre. The gap between Marmont's left and centre was widening rapidly as he pressed on to outflank the Allies. Wellington was gnawing a chicken bone in a distant farmyard. He had already ordered the 3rd Division to come up, and its commander happened to be Pakenham. He threw his bone over the farm wall, gazed through his glass at the French and exclaimed: 'By God! That will do.' Marmont had, in fact, been mortally wounded by a cannon ball from the Lesser Arapile and the French left was split in two. The Duke leapt onto his horse, galloped up the slippery Lesser Arapile and ordered Pakenham to lead the 3rd against the French forthwith. 'I will, my Lord, if you will give me your hand.' Wellington shook hands with his brother-in-law and galloped off to deliver messages to the rest of the staff with equal abruptness. Afterwards, some of the parliamentary Opposition criticised him for dispensing with the usual politesse of formal notes to communicate orders, but the majority were getting to know his style.

Ned Pakenham's lively response won enthusiastic applause from Wellington. Ned may not have been the highest genius but the speed, clearness and accuracy of his understanding were unbeatable. And when Pakenham and his 3rd Division soundly defeated the unhappy French, deprived both of Marmont and their morale, it was a Frenchman who said that Wellington had defeated '40,000 French in forty minutes'.

Salamanca to Vitoria. It sounds a glorious progress and it was – up to a point. Some of Wellington's friends already had Paris in their sights when he decided on a triumphal entry into Madrid, spoilt for him to some extent by having to be kissed by the men as well as the women. In recompense he was presented with the great Spanish order of the Golden Fleece. The Spanish Cortes (Parliament) created him Generalissimo of all their forces, with a grant of £100,000 towards buying a home. The women proclaimed that his mother was a saint and the daughter of a saint. (Lady Mornington had once been threatened with arrest for debt.) But despite all this hallooing, Wellington was by no means out of the woods yet.

It may be that considerations beyond the family's sanctity prompted Arthur's next, surprisingly optimistic, move. He explained in letters to his brother William Wellesley-Pole that he was bound by his success to help the home government. His proposed method of doing so in autumn 1812 was to march north to Valladolid and Burgos, clearing Napoleon's forces out of both until, by December, he could rest on the Ebro, the last great river barrier before the Pyrenees. Valladolid went well; Burgos was another matter: an immensely strong castle, an ominous church on whose altar the black, long-haired Christ wore rhinoceros hide – an infinitely gloomy city. (Over a century later it was not a surprise to hear that Franco's HQ was Burgos.)

Wellington's attempt on and retreat from Burgos was fraught with misery. He lost his favourite and most gallant young officer, Major Edward Somers-Cocks, while rallying his men. After the whole operation was called off to retreat to Ciudad Rodrigo for the winter, things went no better, although Napoleon had begun his even more disastrous retreat from Moscow just three days before Wellington pulled out of Burgos, each of the two curiously similar events bringing its own agonies. Though Napoleon's retreat was more shameful and damaging, it was Wellington who more keenly felt the disgrace when army discipline collapsed and punishments followed. They not only ate pigs' acorns but went out shooting the peasants' pigs, and to go pig-hunting was a military disgrace.

It was at about this period that the image of the 'Iron Duke' began to take shape. He was by no means a hard commander but his occasional outbursts were remembered. 'There is but one way', he wrote, 'to do as I did – to have A HAND OF IRON. The moment there was the slightest neglect in any department I was down on them.' Once in winter quarters Wellington's army recovered and the iron man's mood changed. He had always called himself the Child of Fortune and now he proposed as soon as possible 'to get in Fortune's way'.

Despite the failure at Burgos, for which Wellington ultimately took the blame (he confessed to having attacked Burgos as if it were an Indian hill-fort, whereas it was defended by one of Napoleon's 'very clever' fellows), Cádiz gave its new Generalissimo an ecstatic welcome in early 1813. This hero-worship struck from the 'iron man' (as Ned Pakenham called him) the most characteristic spark of his life: 'I was very well received at Cádiz and Lisbon and throughout the country and I ought to have somebody behind me to remind me that I am "but a man".'

Wellington had been made Colonel of the Blues by the Horse Guards and a Knight of the Garter by the King in 1813 despite Burgos – and the fact that he had not known whether the blue Garter ribbon was worn from the right or left shoulder.

At the end of May 1813 the figure on horseback in his familiar drab grey cloak was raising his plumeless hat in a gesture of 'farewell' to Portugal and 'forward' into

Spain for himself and his army. It would be only two years before the same figure was raising his hat in the same 'forward' gesture – but this time the scene would be the ridge at Waterloo rather than the Spanish–Portuguese frontier.

Three weeks later, on 21 June 1813, Wellington's Allied army of 78,000 men and 70 guns was facing Napoleon's brother, King Joseph of Spain, his army of 57,000 and 80 guns. The two sides were drawn up before the town of Vitoria on its ten-mile diamond-shaped plain lying among hills and cut by the River Zadora and the royal road to France. King Joseph had not resisted the temptation to erect towering stands in the town from which the population could watch him beat Wellington. The town's name, Vitoria, was not to symbolise the King's triumph, however, and victory was the Duke's.

The morning was wet and misty – but after Salamanca rain was assumed to be a sign of a Wellington victory. (It was not to fail him at Waterloo.) The focal point of the struggle was a conical hill where 300 of the Black Prince's knights had once fallen. But this time it was the French who gradually gave way until the cry dreaded by every French army began to be heard: 'Sauve qui peut'. As always after a great battle, whether the result had been moderately good or glorious, Wellington's mood was sombre. He was thinking not of the glory but of the losses.

It may have been in one of these softened moods that Wellington gave his exhausted army permission to rest during the night instead of marching off at once in pursuit of King Joseph, who meanwhile escaped with 35,000 men across the Pyrenees into France. But instead of resting, the soldiers – and a few officers also – helped themselves to the untold wealth scattered in French wagons over the battlefield. They made the most of wine, women and a total of five million dollars in a night-long bacchanalia, looting from the French what the French had earlier looted from the Spanish, so that when Wellington was ready to march at dawn, his army was fit only for drunken sleep.

'The scum of the earth', Wellington called them in a phrase that for years was to blacken his reputation with reformers and others who had been his admirers. It was only in 1831 that he made his true position plain. While arguing in favour of flogging, he explained that the French army, composed of conscripts – 'no matter whether your son or my son' – did not require flogging on the triangle, whereas the British 'volunteer army were not super-patriots but men escaping justice, with bastard children, or seeking cheap wine – the scum of the earth'. Wellington added, significantly, that it was wonderful how the army had made of them 'the fine fellows they are'. Unfortunately the phrase 'scum of the earth' has outlived the phrase 'fine fellows' to the great phrase-maker's detriment.

S I X

INTO FRANCE

The Peninsular War had been waged under Wellington as commander-in-chief for four years and the end was now in sight. First it had been 'Into Portugal' then 'Into Spain', then after a retreat, to Portugal, 'Back to Spain', and finally 'Into France'. Napoleon, calling his brother's defeat in Spain 'ridiculous', replaced King Joseph by Marshal Soult as commander-in-chief, while the Prince Regent created Wellington Britain's first ever field marshal and presented him with the first baton, decorated not with eagles but with lions.

The last stage of the Peninsular War began frustratingly with simultaneous assaults on the Spanish fortresses of Pamplona and San Sebastián, which were so far apart that Wellington could not conduct both operations himself. Yet he had to capture both in order to secure his Spanish frontier with France. Pamplona, associated with the legendary Roland and Roncesvalles, finally fell on 31 October 1813 after the battlefield was temporarily lost in a deep Pyrenean mist. There were some critical moments even after Wellington took over from Cole (4th Division) and Picton (3rd Division) as commander. Marshal Soult was about to cut them off when loud cheering and shouts of 'Nosey! Nosey!' announced that the figure galloping up the ridge above the village of Sorauren was the hero himself. Pamplona, only a few miles ahead, was busy preparing lights and flags to celebrate Marshal Soult's victory. But the Battle of Sorauren was to be the prelude to Wellington's occupation of Pamplona not Soult's. After Sorauren the conqueror's brother William received a letter admitting that Arthur began to feel that 'the hand of God' was upon him: even though it had been 'a close run thing'.

On 31 August 1813 Wellington showed his psychological insight by arranging that Soult's counter-attack on San Marcial, the heights above San Sebastián, should be defeated by the Spanish alone, single-handed. As well as building the confidence of his Allies, his action demonstrates that, contrary to jealous critics, he did not insist on getting all the credit all the time. That very morning of 31 August San Sebastián fell, though General Rey withdrew his troops up Mount Ürgull and into a castle above the town. They held out there until 9 September when the whole garrison was over-whelmed and slaughtered in the most ghastly display of savagery of the whole Peninsular War – even worse than events at Ciudad Rodrigo and Badajoz. Why did not Wellington stamp out these horrors, asked William Napier the historian, by rewarding the good soldiers and shooting the looters on the spot? There was no such quick way out in a period when public opinion expected the common soldier to perform miracles of endurance. The common soldier could screw himself up to the necessary pitch of endurance by banishing pity and fear. When human feelings returned they took the form of pure brutality.*

It was not until 7 October that Wellington's exhausted army was ready to cross into France. But nothing would induce Wellington to hasten the final days of San Sebastián by bombardment, which he said would be 'very inconvenient to our friends the inhabitants and ultimately to ourselves'.

Four great rivers had to be crossed by Wellington's men before they could be said to have forced their way right into France: the Bidassoa, the Nivelle, the Nive and the Adour. But it was 8 August before Wellington was fit to lead a fresh push into the Pyrenees. He had gone down with lumbago after Sorauren and his fifteen chargers were skin and bone with all the riding. A diarist likened him to a centaur – a legendary man-horse – forever glued to his saddle, in which he slept instead of going to bed. He ate little and drank no wine with his friends.

He refused to move forward until the tactically correct moment, despite the clamour from the home

---

* War has its ironies as well as its horrors. In 1925 the Queen of Spain opened a cemetery in a flower garden above San Sebastián commemorating the English who had fallen fighting for Spain, 1813 being the first date on the tombs there. By the 1960s four out of six gunners in a group of statuary had had their heads knocked off while the 'flower garden' was a bed of wild garlic.

press at the delays. Then, in the words of the diarist William Bragge, on 7 October Wellington's army 'infringed upon the Sacred Territory at last' by crossing the River Bidassoa into France.

It was 31 October before Pamplona fell at last, and February 1814 before he heard any good personal news: King Joseph's pictures which the 'scum' had looted after Vitoria turned out to have been originally looted by King Joseph himself, so when Wellington had them shipped to England for return to King Ferdinand of Spain, the grateful Spanish King presented a number of masterpieces among them to the Duke of Wellington. Today they can be seen hanging at Apsley House and Stratfield Saye.

Though everything went smoothly – Pamplona surrendered, its garrison emerging like skeletons from their tombs on resurrection morning, while Wellington held many pleasantly informal discussions with his staff on remote hill-tops – the picture of the Duke presented to the world was again a grim one. This was partly due to the acerbic pen of a famous new Peninsular War diarist, Ensign Rees Howell Gronow. His first impression was of 'a very stern and grave-looking' man with a 'knowing' thoroughbred, Copenhagen. There was no deviation here from the old Wellington of the harsh past, more often than not on the defensive.

November was not far advanced before Wellington's now splendid army seized the second river-line into France by winning the Battle of Nivelles. He was inferior only in one respect: Soult outnumbered him. This was due to the many Spanish soldiers being sent home for plundering the French peasantry just as they themselves had been plundered by the French. But Wellington would not tolerate even tit-for-tat plundering; he needed a friendly countryside and he appointed his brother-in-law Ned to reorganise the military police, which he did, like 'a raving lion'. The only hostile commander who sometimes held back this most effective army was, in William Napier's words, 'General Rain'.

With the spring of 1814 came new advances for the Duke of Wellington's army involving the crossing of fresh river passes and acts of daring by many of his individual commanders – by now the dazzling products of his own successful system of training. Of course there were the setbacks. For instance, after Nivelle, Wellington praised the heroic John Colborne and his 52nd, but added that 'we must not rob but respect the peasants' property', to which Colborne agreed, while adding that in the heat of action there were bound to be 'irregularities'. Wellington's tone immediately recovered its old sharpness: 'Ah! ah! Stop it in future, Colborne'.

His one relaxation for the sake of his health was hunting up in the mountains above the bay, wearing the sky-blue coat given by Lady Salisbury, black cape and 'Wellington boots' – an early specimen of the famous waterproof footwear.

Meanwhile, what was to be the next step now that Europe had defeated Napoleon at Leipzig in Germany? Wellington was thinking all these things over as his army advanced ever eastwards, over mountain pass and river. He drew up reports sitting on a stone under a borrowed umbrella and snatched moments of sleep wrapped in his white winter cloak.

Were these thoughts and his usual method of procedure interrupted for a week by a unique event on 27 February 1814? After defeating Soult at Orthez, he was riding side by side with General Alava, Spanish liaison, on the pursuit when Alava suddenly shouted that he had been hit on the bottom. Wellington laughed; next moment the laughter was silenced by Wellington's coming as near as he ever did to being wounded. A spent bullet hit his sword-hilt, driving it against his thigh and cutting the skin. It was the end of March 1814 before he had recovered enough to gallop again. Wellington had hitherto always attributed his escapes unwounded from great battles either to having been born wearing 'Fortunatus' cap or, more often, to the 'Finger of Providence'. He was, in fact, never even nearly wounded again, so despite his brother William's fear, God had not removed his protective hand.

By April 1814 rumours were flying: Napoleon was dead; the Allies were at loggerheads. Wellington warned his staff to ignore all reports. However, the Allies had signed the Treaty of Chaumont, dated 1 March, to create the Quadruple Alliance and had entered Paris on the 31st. A credible report of the news did not reach Wellington and, unaided by the telegraph or even second sight, the sceptical Duke ordered the assault on Toulouse for 10 April 1814.

The capture of the city was both the closest-run and most unnecessary thing of the whole Peninsular War. Wellington and his Allies lost 4,500 men, 2,300 more than the defeated Soult. During a victory dinner, the full truth and latest news reached Wellington and his friends from Paris: Napoleon had abdicated and as of 6 April Louis XVIII was again King of France. The cheering led by the commander-in-chief with a champagne toast to the King was immediately followed by another champagne toast given by Alava to the saviour of Europe. Wellington looked confused as the shouts rose and roared. He was soon ordering the coffee.

Napoleon had already fallen in two senses before the dinner began. The people had hurled his statue from its crowning position on the Town Hall in Toulouse and in Paris his fate was decided: he was to be an exile on Elba, with a generous pension for his family. There seemed to be only one sceptical voice left in the civilised world. Fanny Burney, the celebrated novelist, sat by her father's bedside in Chelsea, London, watching the fireworks soaring up from the Great Hall where Wellington had stood his trial for Cintra in 1808. Dr Burney was dying but he had not lost his senses. When they told him that Boney was stowed away for ever on the island of Elba, he shrugged his old shoulders sceptically and turned away from the fireworks to the blank wall.

The fun began on 23 June 1814 when the foreign sovereigns arrived in London for a state visit. The crowds were roaring themselves hoarse, but it was

Wellington they longed to see. They planned to lift him out of his carriage, depositing him in the arms of Duchess Kitty at their house in Hamilton Place, Piccadilly. But he was too quick for them. He knew their little ways. Those hoarse hurrahs stood for a British welcome just as those who had been shouting vivas for the last five years stood for different traditions. He slipped past the huzzahs and rode home alone.

He was not so thoroughly British as perhaps he had been five years previously and now he was going back to Paris to be British ambassador at the court of King Louis XVIII. What did Arthur think of that? His brother Henry Wellesley, himself a diplomat, told the Duke that compared with military service, he would find diplomacy 'a very pretty amusement'. And Kitty? One of Wellington's most astute biographers pointed out that Kitty was temperamentally more fit to be the hard-working wife of a vicar and to run a parish than the household of the country's greatest hero, who was now ambassador in one of Europe's first courts. Kitty's private diaries show that she was not assisted by low self-esteem. She despised herself for idleness, and Arthur despised and scolded her for weakly giving the housekeeping money to beggars. They had not met for five years because Arthur had taken no leave from the Peninsula, and it was therefore untrue that he had betrayed Kitty with the notorious London courtesan Harriette Wilson. Harriette's publisher threatened to incriminate Wellington in her forthcoming memoirs unless he bought her silence; Arthur had not visited

Harriette since his marriage and his reply was unforgettable: 'Publish and be damned.' But there were other ladies. And Kitty, while exceptionally kind to any of Arthur's relatives who might appeal for help, added little to the ambassadorial court. For one thing, though short-sighted, she would not wear spectacles in her carriage and so could not recognise those who kindly saluted her.

Kitty continued to adore and fear her Arthur. Europe, having acclaimed him as a great soldier, whether in Lisbon, Madrid, Paris or London, was now about to get the chance to respect him as an effective diplomat. But before plunging into the sensational events centred around the Congress of Vienna, it is important to see in the round the hero as he appeared so far. 'See the Conquering Hero Comes', sang the crowds. His admirer, the military historian William Napier, saw in him a leader of 'genius'. He gave his men unique confidence so that they became his 'model army', no longer 'scum'. Did they see anything that could be improved in their hero? Two things perhaps. Every leader, whether military or political, must strike a balance between being communicative and being silent. Wellington erred on the side of silence. He had no urge to take his comrades into his confidence; in fact he had already made his position clear long ago in India – 'I like to walk alone.' Following closely on that point was a tendency to withhold praise even when praise was due. He was no chatterer, no flatterer. Was this a little inhuman, or rather, as the majority of his men saw it, godlike?

His Grace the Duke of Wellington, KG, arrived in Paris as British ambassador on 24 August 1814 and bought a magnificent embassy for his government. It had belonged to Princess Pauline Borghese, Napoleon's sister; its garden ran down to the Champs Elysées and was itself an Elysian spot. Clever and beautiful women began to play a part in Wellington's life as never before: Madame de Staël, the brilliant writer, Giuseppina Grassini (the singer who had transferred her favours from Bonaparte to his conqueror) and Dorothea, the niece of Talleyrand and the French politician's hostess in Vienna where the peace conference assembled in September 1814. There was also Mademoiselle Georges who claimed the 'protection' of both Napoleon and Wellington, adding 'Mais M. le duc etait de beaucoup le plus fort' – 'But the Duke was much the stronger'. After the great Paris days were over, a lady asked him if it was true that he had received all that female adulation. He replied with his usual frankness: 'Oh yes! Plenty of that! Plenty of that!'

There was also plenty of the other – plenty of the criticism and animosity that was the opposite of admiration and represented the hostility of the Bonapartists. At the end of October some Bonapartist bullets actually whistled past Wellington and the Duke of Angoulême during a review on the Champs de Mars, and if Arthur could have seen his friend General Foy's diary for these days his anxiety would not have abated. Foy reserved for his diary the hard feelings about the Bourbons and England which had begun to rack him.

Napoleon, as Foy had just heard, was very gay and active on Elba, thinking seriously of regaining his crown. If Foy, an honourable man who liked Wellington personally, felt like this, the Ambassador was clearly in trouble. Alarmed for the Duke's safety, the British government finally decided that their hero must leave the dangers of Paris for a time and join the politicians in Vienna to discuss a peace treaty.

Lord Castlereagh, the Tory Foreign Secretary, was persuaded to return to his work in England from Vienna so that Wellington could take his place at the Congress. As usual Wellington refused to leave his job by the back door. He had insisted long ago on leaving Portugal by the front, and now he began a diplomatic career which was praised by Talleyrand: 'He never indulged in that parade of mystification which is generally employed by Ambassadors: watchfulness, prudence and experience of human nature, were the only means he employed.' Wellington changed every night on the long drive to Vienna, although his aides kept on their crumpled day clothes – after all the 'Beau' was the 'Beau'. At Vienna he found that peace-making was often just merry-making. He settled down to practise two opposites: calm always balanced by alertness.

Events on Elba were neither calm nor alert. Bonaparte's governors were well aware of four facts, but were not prepared to act on any of them. First, Bonaparte knew all about the disputes at the Congress over the new Europe; second, the ex-emperor's grant had not been paid; third, Bonaparte feared assassination;

Fourth, he had said he would have to take the field again. They took no action except that one of them, Sir Neil Campbell, decided to go to the mainland on 16 February; he courteously told his captive of his plans and promised to return for a party on the island on the 28th. There was also a prediction. Napoleon had foretold that he would be returning to France with the violets of spring.

Now it was 7 March and Dorothea was planning the rehearsal of a light-hearted comedy as she sat on the end of her uncle Talleyrand's bed while his hair was perfumed. Wellington had summoned his horse, for he intended to enjoy an invigorating spring ride. He sent it back to the stable, for on 7 March the news came through that another horse had bolted: Napoleon had escaped from Elba.

SEVEN

THE DUCHESS OF RICHMOND'S BALL

Lord Liverpool, the Tory Prime Minister, gave Wellington a choice. Would he face Napoleon as a diplomat – his present service – or would he return to command the army? Tsar Alexander of Russia, who was with the Duke in Vienna, had no question to put. He simply laid his hand on the Duke's shoulder and said: 'It is for you to save the world again.' Wellington had once called Napoleon 'The Grand Disturber'. The ex-emperor must now be faced by 'The Man of Iron'.

It was hard to believe that serious events were happening at last. After all, the Whig *Morning Chronicle* had been describing the politics of the Congress as one long holiday:

> We learn from high sources a project is made,
> How Vienna's grand Congress the Christmas
>   will spend.
> Since public affairs have so long been delayed
> They may very well wait till the holidays end.

Would it all be taken more seriously now that Marshal Ney had changed sides again? After swearing that he would bring Bonaparte to Paris in a cage, Ney was now once more a Bonapartist.

Wellington joined Congress in outlawing Napoleon and became commander-in-chief of the British–Dutch–Belgian forces in Flanders. Napoleon was carried into the Tuileries Palace with his eyes closed and a sleep-walker's smile on his face. Less than a month later, on 4 April, Wellington entered Brussels, the centre-point of his Allied army, while the Rothschild brothers were to fund him with over a quarter of a million pounds in gold and cash.

The Hundred Days, as Napoleon's new period of power was to be called, was nearly a third of the way through and still there was no solution to the knottiest problems. Who was to be the Allies' choice for a new hereditary king of France? Wellington wanted an alternative to both Bonapartists and 'rock-bottom Bourbons'. Louis Philippe, Duke of Orléans, seemed to be his man, but in fact was not to rule France until 1830 – another fifteen years away. Then there was the problem of who was to command the Allied armies. The Prince of Orange, who as 'slender Billy' had served in the Peninsular War, had to serve under Wellington. He agreed reluctantly.

There were, of course, rivalries among the British generals, too. General Ned Pakenham, alas, had been removed from the field by death at the Battle of New Orléans. To some people, Lord Uxbridge, the future Marquess of Anglesey, seemed to have removed himself by having eloped with Henry Wellesley's wife. But

Wellington had to choose the best man for the job and this was undoubtedly Uxbridge. Why did not the government call out the militia? And where, oh where was his Peninsula army? As Wellington wrote on 8 May 1815, they were 'very weak and ill equipped', 'an infamous army'.

Surprisingly, Kitty Wellington, who had lost her favourite brother Ned, was one of the Duke's most effective spokesmen in London, raising morale with words like: 'Ah! wait a little, he is in his element now, depend on him.'

When Wellington's old acquaintance Thomas Creevey asked him about the coming battle, he replied: 'By God! I think Blücher and myself can do the thing.' Creevey went on to hint that there would be many desertions from Napoleon to the Allies. 'Not upon a man', said Wellington, 'from the colonel to the private . . . inclusive' – though on second or third thoughts, they might 'pick up a marshal or two, perhaps; but not worth a damn'. Just then, remembered Creevey, a British infantryman, came in sight, peering about at the Park and its statuary. 'There', said Wellington, pointing to the small scarlet figure. 'There, it all depends upon that article whether we do the business or not. Give me enough of it, and I am sure.' Wellington was making amends for 'infamous' and 'scum'.

With the end of May and the beginning of June Wellington had to face a period of intense, conflicting rumours. When would Napoleon cross the frontier?

On 6 June British intelligence was unanimous that Bonaparte was approaching the frontier towards Lille. Wellington advised Lady Georgiana Lennox to dissuade her mother the Duchess of Richmond from picnicking at Lille or Tournai on 8 June as she planned. Yet Napoleon was still in Paris on 8 June. By the 13th, Wellington was assuming that the 'Grand Disturber' did not intend to disturb them for quite a while. In fact, he had left Paris the day before. Wellington's intelligence department was not one of his army's strong points.

Another 'disturber' in a somewhat different mode was Wellington's friend and ally, the Prussian commander. Wellington admired him as a 'fine fellow', although he suffered from occasional mental disturbance; in 1811 he believed himself to be pregnant of an elephant. Wellington had met Blücher between Brussels and Liège on 3 May to concert their joint strategy. It was settled that the British–Dutch–Belgian army should keep their frontier fortresses secure to prevent an outflanking movement by Napoleon towards the west, while ready, if necessary, to move towards the Prussians at the centre.

An advance Prussian patrol failed to notify Wellington that on the night of 13–14 June they had sighted the flickering of innumerable camp-fires near Beaumont on the French side of the River Sambre. Meanwhile, hundreds of Bonapartist broadsheets had already flooded Belgium, offering the faithful the triple crown of glory, liberty and loot. No wonder the Allies' intelligence failed them; for Napoleon had sealed the Sambre and

Moselle frontiers as only he knew how. From 7 June, a full week before Waterloo, not a fishing-boat was allowed to move and no information except false rumours was allowed to pass across. On the 12th at 3.30 a.m. Bonaparte left Paris for Beaumont, his headquarters; on the 14th he was addressing his soldiers on hopes of future glory based on memories of the glorious past.

Wellington was receiving more concrete support than mere memories could provide. His bootmaker, the famous Hoby of St James's Street, London, had just sent him the two new pairs of 'Wellington boots', so urgently requested. Both the other two pairs had been an inch or two too small in length of leg and breadth of calf. Hoby, a Methodist preacher as well as shopkeeper, attributed the Duke's successes to his own prayers and boots. Wellington believed in the 'Finger of Providence', Hoby in the foot. If ever both were necessary, it was now.

The Duke was also concerned with conducting the best possible psychological warfare. The Allies' confidence together with British phlegm could be dramatically presented by scarlet uniforms, cricket matches, pink champagne, dancing . . . As the Duke had himself once said: 'Plenty of that! Plenty of that!' In particular there was plenty of light-hearted flirtation. Again the Duke was to the fore. He was spotted one day disappearing into a tree-screened green hollow with the beautiful Lady Frances Wedderburn-Webster. There might have been plenty more of that, but for the fact that Frances was shortly expecting a baby. When he was warned not to invite Lady John Campbell to his house by one of his staff because her character was suspected of being 'loose', he retorted: 'Is it, by —? Then I will go and ask her myself.'

Where did Napoleon intend to strike? Long before dawn on 15 June Napoleon began his advance into Belgium. At about 3 p.m. Wellington received the first report: the Prussians had been attacked at Charleroi. But were these assaults only feints with the real action elsewhere? The answer – contrary to Wellington's expectations – was no. Napoleon's plan was not for a lethal sweep cutting the Allies off on their right, but a crushing blow at the centre. It was time for the very greatest act of psychological warfare – a really grand ball. The army would concentrate at Quatre Bras and Nivelles while the Duchess of Richmond held her long-planned ball in Brussels. At 5 a.m. the dancers would march in good time for Quatre Bras.

It was while Wellington was actually dressing for the ball that he received alarming news: that very afternoon there had been a close-run thing at Quatre Bras. Prince Bernhard of Saxe-Weimar on his own initiative had brilliantly cleared the Quatre Bras crossroads of French skirmishers. When Marshal Ney rode up it was only the tall fields of rye that prevented him seeing the open road into Brussels. Why did not Wellington cancel the ball or at least ride to Quatre Bras himself? His place was in Brussels; he feared a stab in the back from local Bonapartists and the ball was a morale-builder and convenient gathering place for all his officers.

And so he rode to the most famous ball in history, incidentally enabling the poet Byron and the novelist Thackeray to send Childe Harold and Becky Sharp to the same party:

> There was a sound of revelry by night
> And Belgium's Capital had gather'd then
> Her Beauty and her Chivalry – and bright
> The lamps shone o'er fair women and brave men.

Becky in a pink ball-dress flashed her green eyes; Lady Dalrymple-Hamilton sat by Wellington on a sofa and noticed that his gaiety was punctured by strange signs of anxiety; the beautiful Lady Charlotte Greville, on his arm on the way into supper, saw him handed a despatch, unopened, by the Prince of Orange; and the Prince left the ball without waiting for supper. At supper he reappeared and whispered a long message, then left again. Officers slipped away afterwards. They were to reappear on the field in their dancing pumps.

At last the time had come to close the ball without suspicion. After his goodbyes, Wellington turned to his host, Richmond, Had Richmond a good map in the house? As they sat before a map in the study, Wellington burst out: 'Napoleon has *humbugged me*, by God!' He had stolen a march of twenty-four hours on the Allies and they would have to fight him at Quatre Bras. But they would not stop him there. And pressing his thumb on a position just south of Waterloo, the Duke said: 'I must fight him here.' Then he slipped away to bed for an hour or so, for once not leaving by the hall door.

It was a unique scene of discomfiture, and may have provoked a famous question and answer. Did not anxiety make him lie awake at night? 'I don't like lying awake, it does no good. I make a point never to lie awake.' This was a typically Wellingtonian cure for insomnia. So he slept soundly through the rising tumult of war-cries – pipes, drums, bugles – till 4 a.m., when he rode out to lead his army at Quatre Bras, the crossroads that was now the crux. As he passed under the window of Lady Dalrymple-Hamilton's lodgings her maid caught sight of him: 'Oh my lady, get up quick; there he goes, God bless him, and he will not come back till he is King of France!'

Wellington found a curious situation at Quatre Bras when he trotted in at 10 a.m. The Prince of Orange was lying low until the reinforcements he had sent for had arrived, for the Dutch–Belgians were outnumbered three to one by Marshal Ney's force. The Duke therefore decided to ride over to Bussy windmill where he and Blücher could concert their joint plans.

They climbed the mill together. And what a sight met their telescopes. Bonaparte and his staff were clearly visible, gazing up at them. Indeed, the three army commanders were probably training their telescopes on one another at the same moment. The Duke noticed with alarm that the 84,000 Prussians were drawn up at

Ligny brook on the forward slope, instead of on the reverse slope, according to his own new style that had won him the Peninsular War. As tactfully as possible, he warned Blücher that British troops would expect to be beaten in such an exposed position. 'My men like to see their enemy', replied Gneisenau, Blücher's second-in-command.

As Wellington re-entered the crossroads at 2.20 p.m., nine cannon shots rang out in his rear. It was the signal for the Battle of Ligny to begin. At the same time, the Duke recognised the jingle a few miles away that always heralded a French advance: 'L'Empereur recompensera celui qui s'avancera!' – 'The Emperor will reward anyone who advances!' It was Marshal Ney about to attack Quatre Bras. As it turned out, the Battle of Quatre Bras had a dramatic pattern of its own, each side having a strange *deus ex machina* working on its behalf, so that both French and English were found claiming the ultimate victory at the crossroads.

At 2.20 p.m. on 16 June Wellington was in a fairly grim situation: only 7,000 men to Ney's 20,000 and a desperate weakness in guns, ammunition, cavalry. But almost at once Picton's division had descended as it were from the clouds, followed by more and more godlike reinforcements, until the Allies had built up to 36,000 while Ney remained at 20,000. Ney's *deus ex machina* was to have been Marshal d'Erlon, but he emerged as a false god. Time and again Ney sent for d'Erlon; each time d'Erlon set out as arranged but was stopped in his tracks by a counter-message from Ligny to turn right about and bestow his help there. D'Erlon spent the whole day marching between the two battlefields, Quatre Bras and Ligny, without firing a shot on either.

Wellington had suffered many grievous casualties. The young Duke of Brunswick, sent to rally some young Netherlanders and Belgians who were falling back in Bossu wood, was shot dead. He was the brother of Princess Caroline of Wales. Wellington himself had a narrow escape. He had to gallop for his life, skimming a ditch lined with Picton's Highlanders and their bayonets. 'Ninety-second, lie down!' he shouted as he took off. A worse horse and a worse rider, said Fitzroy Somerset, his aide-de-camp, would not have come through.

Wellington had a fresh Hanoverian division (trained in England) to throw in; but Ney had the inspiration of frustration and fury. After 5 p.m. he managed to force a handful of Kellerman's cavalry onto the crossroads and it needed a bloody massacre by Halkett's muskets and the Gordons to dispose of them. Once Wellington had his 36,000 men, including the Guards, his anxieties were over. At 6.30 the bugles sounded the advance and by 9 p.m., as darkness fell, the battle was over. It was Wellington who re-entered Brussels, not Ney.

Wellington had gloomily predicted that Blücher would be 'damnably mauled' at Ligny – and he was; both his army and himself. His army was in full retreat towards the east and Blücher, having been thrown and ridden over, lay battered and bruised in a cottage, kept alive by gin and rhubarb. As he said, 'Ich stinke etwas –

'I stink somewhat'. In fact Blücher and his Prussians had fallen back eighteen miles to Wavre – and as they had fallen back, Wellington and the Allies must fall back too. So said the Duke. Napoleon was not going to drive a wedge between them so easily. It was not the least of Blücher's victories that he defeated Gneisenau's suggestions after Ligny for parting company with the Allies and making off north-eastwards.

Already months previously Wellington had made his engineers prospect the land south of Brussels and they knew the Forest of Soignes and the ridge of Waterloo. He would stand and fight – if Blücher would support him, 'even with one corps only'.

At 1 o'clock on Saturday 17 June Napoleon was suddenly aroused from a somewhat lethargic morning by an astounding report. Quatre Bras village was empty and Wellington, whom he intended to capture forthwith, had vanished. Napoleon gave Ney an acid look and said in front of d'Erlon, 'On a perdu la France' – 'France is lost'.

Wellington, meanwhile, with a cheerful carefree pose as studied as it was successful, had led his army into a retreat parallel with the Prussians at Wavre. Wellington's location by the afternoon of the 17th was the ridge below the Waterloo ridge itself. The main road cut through this second ridge, on which stood an inn, La Belle-Alliance. It was here that he intended to stand and fight next day. There was no need to rush or to spoil his proverbial calm. Napoleon had discovered his departure too late. And the weather was against him.

One question, however, does remain: which ridge south of Waterloo did Wellington mean to occupy? The first, facing south, or the second, facing north? It has always been assumed that the Duke personally picked the ridge facing south and west and never deviated in his intention. But when Fitzroy Somerset's diary was examined by the present author, a somewhat different story emerged. Somerset, a most accurate reporter, described how the Duke ordered de Lancey, his quartermaster general, to mark out the Belle-Alliance position (facing across the plain to Waterloo). De Lancey found it was too 'extended' for the Allied army to cope with, so he marked out the more northerly ridge, leaving La Belle-Alliance to Napoleon. Of course it would not have been uncharacteristic of Wellington to keep the details flexible and the final plan secret. After all, the two ridges enclosed the same battlefield, though facing opposite ways.

Two other well-known anecdotes throw typical light on Wellington's mood before the battle. Wellington and his army had quietly mounted Waterloo ridge, the Duke deliberately entering his headquarters in the village without creating any stir. Wishing to know more of his opponents' situation, Napoleon challenged them by firing some batteries. Unfortunately, the Allied batteries responded and thus revealed what was being kept dark. It was Wellington, now in no sweet temper, whom Lord Uxbridge later approached to enquire about his strategy. (Uxbridge, the future Lord Anglesey, was the one who had run off with Henry Wellesley's wife; he would also become commander-in-chief if the Finger of Providence suddenly left Wellington to his fate.) In answer to Uxbridge's question about his intentions, the Duke snapped back: 'Who will attack the first tomorrow, I or Bonaparte?' 'Bonaparte', Uxbridge replied. Wellington then drew the obvious angry conclusion: if his plan depended on Bonaparte's, how could he answer Uxbridge's question in advance? Suddenly, as so often before, a burst of bad temper was immediately wiped out. Wellington jumped up, laid his hand on Uxbridge's shoulder and said: 'There is one thing certain, Uxbridge, that is, that whatever happens, you and I will do our duty.'

Henry House, the famous French historian, suggests that far from doing his duty by his army, Wellington was an arch-gambler who went into the Battle of Waterloo without any firm assurance of essential Prussian support. But later evidence, particularly from Fitzroy Somerset and Müffling, his Prussian liaison officer, shows that as usual the Duke had left nothing to chance. He sent a message to Blücher on the night of 17 June to say that he was in position on Mont-Saint-Jean to do battle next day, provided he was guaranteed the presence of at least one or two Prussian corps. Old Blücher was able to reply that Gneisenau had given way and the support was promised. Wellington received the message in the early hours of the 18th – at 6 a.m. according to Somerset.

In later days the Duke was to compare the French with the Allied arms in a famous simile: Napoleon's army was like a splendid harness, perfect for its purpose, but if it broke, no good; Wellington's army was like a rope, broken in places and knotted together, but if it broke yet again, it could still always be knotted. The rope had been knotted after Quatre Bras and Ligny. It was ready to take the strain again.

EIGHT

WATERLOO

Wellington rode out at 6 a.m. on the morning of Sunday 18 June 1815 on his chestnut horse, Copenhagen, who had carried him to victory from Vitoria to Toulouse. He turned to Müffling who rode at his side: 'Now Napoleon will see how a general of sepoys can defend a position.' He was riding to defend the Château of Hougoumont on the ridge of Mont-Saint-Jean and thinking of Napoleon's sarcastic jokes about the young Arthur Wellesley who was trained in India and only fit to command sepoys. The sepoy general had not done badly so far. The sepoy general had seen Napoleon at Ligny. Now he was to face him at Waterloo.

But at this early hour all both behind and in front of Wellington seemed as gloomy and tearful as the weeping skies. His French landlady in his Waterloo hostelry was in tears of fright. Wellington had clapped her cheerfully on the back: no French person should suffer that day except the French soldiers. In Brussels, vindictive rumours were circulating that Wellington had already been defeated. From midnight onwards one young Englishwoman had to listen to a loud hammering in the hotel room next to hers. It was the nails going into the Duke of Brunswick's coffin. She bravely reminded herself that Wellington had been despaired of before now — at Torres Vedras, for example. Another young lady, however, feared that 'Our Great Hero' was done for. The Duc de Berry had fled to Antwerp the moment he heard Wellington's appeal for calm at Brussels. There seemed a danger that Antwerp would attract a mob of refugees.

As for the troops, both sides had spent a miserable night in torrential rain. One army surgeon slept in a drain that gradually flooded. In the morning the fields were a mass of soft mud. This did not benefit Napoleon. As for the Duke's good spirits, he had testified to his faith in the British soldier a few weeks before Waterloo, and what he had said then still held good.

As Wellington rode along the Mont-Saint-Jean at six o'clock on that midsummer morning, it became obvious that the French across the valley were massing for a head-on frontal attack on the ridge. Yet all along, Wellington had believed firmly that Bonaparte would concentrate on outflanking the Allies on their right and cutting them off from Brussels. For this reason he still left a relatively large force of 1,700 men out on the right at Hal. Why did he do it? First, because he could never believe that Napoleon would be so mad as to challenge head-on that flower of fighters, the British infantryman. Second, because the political effect on Brussels of a turning movement could be extremely serious. Bonaparte committed both these errors while Wellington made a mistake in believing Napoleon could not be so mistaken. In fact, Bonaparte went further still in error. Not only did he think that the British were bad soldiers but he also considered Wellington a bad general. When Marshal Soult tried to dissuade Napoleon from colliding head-on, Napoleon replied that Soult respected Wellington only because he had been beaten by him. On the contrary, the odds were vastly in favour of the French. Another of Napoleon's gnomic phrases that was to have an unfortunate result was among his orders to Marshal Grouchy, who was in command of his most important reinforcements. Grouchy was commanded to 'head for Wavre' (towards which the Prussians had retreated after Ligny) 'to the sound of guns'. Unfortunately for Grouchy, the 'sound of guns' was coming from the Waterloo direction when he heard it, and in marching on Wavre he was marching away from the sound of guns. Grouchy's staff begged him to turn half-left and march westward, Grouchy refused. He insisted on Napoleon's magic signal, 'Wavre'. And so, like d'Erlon before him, by obeying Napoleon slavishly rather than intelligently, he deprived the French of part of their support.

Wellington was standing by the Guards when the struggle for Hougoumont opened. He had ridden along the sunken road on the crest of the ridge, dispensing confidence as Napoleon's orders had dispensed confusion. Two war diarists were to note that Wellington rode 'as if for pleasure' with his alert expression, plain smart uniform, no plumes but the four cockades of Britain, Spain, Portugal and the Netherlands in his hat worn fore and aft.

Bonaparte wore his plumed hat from side to side. His brother Prince Jerome was in command of the attack on Hougoumont, greedy for glory. He had seized some coppices and the orchard and now, at about 11.30 a.m., was up to the walls. Streams of bullets came through every hole in the walls and inner building, until Wellington himself positioned Bull's battery of howitzers immediately behind the château, trusting them to fire on the French over the heads of the Allied infantry, who were then able to drive the attackers off with rifle fire. Hougoumont was again secure, but Jerome would not let go. With fresh troops, the French forced the great gate and wild hand-to-hand battles for possession broke out inside, until five Coldstreamers – four officers and one sergeant – slowly, slowly pushed back the gate. Wellington wrote afterwards: 'The success of the battle of Waterloo depended on the closing of the gates of Hougoumont.' One of the forceful five was Henry Wyndham, and a legend grew up in the Wyndham family that after closing the gates of Hougoumont no Wyndham ever shut another door.

Jerome's assaults had been repulsed a third time by 1 o'clock, this despite his having summoned two extra divisions to one extra Allied brigade. It was time for Wellington to move eastwards along the ridge towards the crossroads of Mont-Saint-Jean.

Before the second act of the great drama could begin, there was a scare off-stage. Napoleon and his staff, gathered at Rossomme, a dominating position, decided to sweep the eastern hills with telescopes before they were obscured by smoke. They all saw it over by Chapelle-Saint-Lambert – a cloud-shadow? a line of trees? Bonaparte realised at once it was the Prussian vanguard – in fact, Bülow's IVth corps. The odds had shortened, perhaps, but could d'Erlon and Ney save the day?

The diarist Edmund Wheatley watched the French infantry winding down the slopes opposite and shivered. These 'gloomy bodies' had something supernatural about them. But they were all too solidly human for their own good. Forgetting the lessons of Bussaco, for instance, they formed into thick, wide, deep phalanxes, too cumbrous ever to deploy. Nevertheless, Wheatley's anxiety was not altogether unjustified. The first onslaught on La Haye Sainte isolated the valiant Germans defending it; even then the French could not actually overrun the farm. D'Erlon's infantry went on to drive Prince Bernhard's men out of Papelotte farm and the 95th Rifles from their protective gravel pit. The Dutch–Belgians, having lost every one of their senior officers, either killed or wounded, withdrew into the Forest of Soignes. At least as Wellington himself conceded, they did not desert to the enemy.

Meanwhile, a crisis was developing on the crest of the ridge where Sir Thomas Picton commanded the splendid infantry, who were only waiting for the order to spring up and dash forward under their two Peninsular leaders, Sir Denis Pack and Sir James Kempt. Picton gave the order and the Gordons, Black Watch and

44th were all in it, though at tragic cost. Picton led Kempt's front line himself: 'Charge! Hurrah! Hurrah!' He was a gallant, eccentric figure, waving his sword and wearing his battle top-hat to protect his eyes. The Gordons staggered under d'Erlon's mass and Picton roared again to Kempt: 'Rally the Highlanders!' They were his last words. Next moment he fell stone dead off his horse, a bullet having pierced his hat and hit him on the temple. The hole can still be seen in one of England's most famous toppers, displayed in the National Army Museum.

From the elm tree he used as his command-post on the ridge Wellington could now see that Picton's men would be overwhelmed if they did not receive immediate fresh support, and so there followed the most exciting and romantic, most often painted episode of the Battle of Waterloo – the Charge of the Heavy Brigade. Everyone connected with that historic charge seemed to be gripped by a touch of madness, from the old, retired Duke of Richmond – who suddenly popped and shouted 'Go along, my boys! Now's your time!' – to the line of great grey horses, to Colonel Fuller who led the Royals shouting 'to Paris!', up to the cavalry commander himself, Lord Uxbridge, who galloped off with the very first horses, instead of staying behind to throw in the reserves if it became necessary.

The French horses who opposed them were altogether lighter in build, and many had been standing out all night with troopers on their backs. 'Those terrible grey horses,' shuddered Napoleon as he watched them pounding across the valley, 'how they fight!' But it is perhaps Corporal Dickson of the Scots Greys and his mare Rattler who have left us the best picture of how they fought: 'I felt a strange thrill run through me [wrote Dickson] and I am sure my noble beast felt the same, for after rearing a moment, she sprang forward, uttering loud neighings and snortings, and leapt over the holly hedge [along the ridge road] at a terrific speed.' Soon she was biting and tearing her way forward with the rest, until she finally dropped to earth from her many wounds. Dickson was suddenly cut off, lucky to burst through into his own lines on a riderless horse, and even to be reunited with a chastened Rattler. Where were those 'strange thrills' now? Uxbridge's cavalry captured two French eagles and disabled fifteen guns from Bonaparte's great battery. Out of Dickson's 300 comrades only thirty returned and sixteen out of twenty-four officers were missing.

A moment was coming in the battle when Wellington would be in desperate need of heavy cavalry. He was to call Waterloo 'the nearest-run thing' and we are now beginning to see why. True, it would soon be mid-afternoon and Napoleon had by no means scented victory. Though the British and Dutch–Belgians had lost 4,500 infantry and 2,500 cavalry, d'Erlon's great attack had failed. Moreover, Papelotte and the gravel pit were again in Wellington's hands, while his two great bastions, Hougoumont and La Haye Sainte, still held firm. Indeed, at about 3 p.m., Hougoumont appeared to have been saved by little short of a miracle. The farm buildings and finally the château itself together with its chapel had been set on fire by French howitzers. The wounded on both sides, the horses in their stables, all were burnt to death. The flames were racing up the chapel but they stopped suddenly. They were at the foot of the cross. The peasants called it miraculous.

Now it was the turn of La Haye Sainte. Napoleon sharply ordered Marshal Ney and his cavalry to assault the ridge and capture it. Wellington had caught his first glimpse of the Prussian vedettes (scouts) at about 2.30 p.m. They could not come too quickly for him. But he was not expecting a miracle. Simply the fulfilment of Blücher's promise.

3.45–6 p.m.

Ney's idea was for a horde of light cavalry, following up the most terrible cannonade the world had yet seen, which forced Wellington to withdraw some of his infantry a hundred yards. This partial retreat emboldened Ney to send in a torrent of 4,500 light cavalry without bothering about cover. Suddenly the foremost cavalry began to laugh as they emerged from the veil of black smoke in the valley, their cuirasses glittering, for the British gunners opposing them seemed to be running away leaving their guns behind. 'The English are done for!' shouted Napoleon's delighted staff. 'Their general is an ignoramus. Look! they are leaving their guns.'

The Duke of Wellington and his charger Copenhagen, by Sir David Wilkie.

Kitty – Catherine Pakenham, Duchess of Wellington, engraving after a drawing by Sir Thomas Lawrence.

Porcelain tureen from the Prussian Dinner Service. The service is decorated with scenes from Wellington's life and was presented to the Duke by King Frederick William of Prussia. This image shows the Battle of Roliça, 17 August 1808.

'Achilles in the Sulks after his Retreat or, The Great Captain on the Stool of Repentance', published by G. Humphrey in 1827. The cartoon shows Wellington after his unexpected resignation as Commander-in-Chief of the Army. Behind Wellington is the statue of Achilles which was visible from his home, Apsley House. It was made from the metal of French guns.

(*Opposite*): *The Battle of Waterloo, 18 June 1815*, by G. Newton. Congreve rockets fly as the sun begins to sink late on the day of the battle. On the left is La Belle-Alliance, La Haye Sainte is in the centre with the Observatory above and Wellington's elm tree is on the right. Hougoumont burns on the horizon.

Queen Victoria and the Marchioness of Douro seated in a carriage attended by the Duke of Wellington, Prince Albert and Sir Robert Peel in Windsor Great Park, 1845, by Henry Barraud.

The First of May, 1851, by Franz Xaver Winterhalter. Wellington presents a gift to his godson, Prince Arthur, who is held by his mother Queen Victoria. Prince Albert stands in the background.

The funeral of the Duke of Wellington passing the archway at Apsley House, his London home, on 18 November 1852, by Louis Haghe, engraved by Thomas Picken.

But Napoleon had not studied Wellington's new tactics, even though they had accounted for the triumphs in the Peninsula. In this third act of the drama at Waterloo the infantry formed squares on or behind the crest, while the gunners were ordered to fire up to the last moment and then immobilise their guns by bowling a wheel of each with them as they retreated inside the British squares. When the French light cavalry were only thirty yards from the summit, volleys of musketry from the squares created a hell of falling riders, toppling horses and riderless steeds to make confusion more confounded.

The squares appeared unmoved from the outside but inside all was horror – dead; wounded in field hospitals, swimming blood as the survivors dragged their stricken comrades into relative safety. Wellington himself ordered fresh cavalry forward whenever he saw an opening. At last Ney called off his shattered columns and Wellington asked one of his aides-de-camp the time. It was 4.20 p.m. 'The battle is mine', said the Duke, 'and if the Prussians arrive soon, there will be an end to the war.'

The Duke was everywhere: he was remembered making a dash to safety when a break in the smoke veil suddenly revealed him on Copenhagen, beckoning the Horse Guards forward with his hat, taking refuge in the 73rd's square as the cuirassiers arrived, welcoming Mercer's G 'Troop' at Hougoumont – 'Ah! that's the way I like to see horse-artillery move.' All agreed there was no one who could restore a shaky battleline like the Duke.

Between 5.30 and 6 o'clock the thing that Wellington had long foreseen took place. Ney at last attacked with a mixed force of 6,000 cavalry and infantry instead of cavalry alone. Now, if ever, the Duke needed his 'heavies'; but they were dead in the valley or within the enemy lines, while the present 'young gentlemen' of the Cumberland Hussars had come for show not action and promptly bolted to Brussels shouting that the French were on their heels. The regiment was afterwards disbanded.

Napoleon, striding up and down outside La Belle-Alliance across the valley, realised that, with the British and Dutch–Belgians in his front and the Prussians on his flank, his chances were down to ten to one against. But he would seize that one chance. Ney must capture La Haye Sainte

6–6.30 p.m.

The heroic defenders of La Haye Sainte, all members of the King's German Legion and commanded by a British major, George Baring, were down to four or five rounds of ammunition each, their ammunition wagon having probably blown up on the way to supply them. The building that had so long been Wellington's bastion inevitably fell, leaving his centre at the mercy of the French, unless fresh troops could be found.

But the Allied bastion had already become a nest of French sharp-shooters and the Duke's aide-de-camp, Fitzroy Somerset, had lost his right arm – he was riding beside the Duke at the time, his left arm actually touching the Duke's right – with nothing between them but the Finger of Providence. Wellington was running short of aides-de-camp. When one of those odd appendages to a nineteenth-century battlefield, a commercial traveller, asked Wellington, 'Anything for Todd and Morrison?' Wellington deftly used him as a substitute aide-de-camp: 'No: but will you do me a service? Go to that officer [pointing along the ridge] and tell him to refuse a flank.'

His second-line battalions were unreliable and when General Halkett asked for reinforcements the answer was 'impossible', which Halkett at once accepted: 'We'll stand till the last man falls.' As Wellington looked at the crawling hands of his watch yet again, someone heard him say: 'Night or the Prussians must come . . .'

6.30– 7 p.m.

With Wellington's centre crumbling, Bonaparte's generals, all eager to deliver the *coup de grâce*, were clamouring for reinforcements from the still untouched fourteen battalions of the Imperial Guard. The Emperor turned down Ney: 'Troops? Where do you expect me to find them? Do you expect me to make them?' With this lie Bonaparte threw away his one chance of victory.

Wellington's task was more complicated, his situation always on the brink and once nearly over it. A Prussian officer informed General Zieten, commander of Blücher's 1st Corps, that Wellington was withdrawing.

Though already about to enter the battlefield, Zieten would have headed back for Blücher but for the lightning descent of Müffling, Wellington's German liaison officer, who sent the Prussians back into action.

On the battered ridge French bombs were still exploding. Wellington and his courageous staff rode up and down, now calling on the groups of terrified young soldiers not to do anything rash, now urging raw recruits and veteran survivors to stand firm a little longer. The young ones wanted action at all costs – 'Let us give them Brummegum!' they shouted, brandishing their bayonets of Birmingham steel. To them Wellington replied: 'Wait a little longer, my lads, you shall have at them presently.'

The men had asked if they were to stand and be massacred and many of the Duke's noblest officers were indeed killed: Colonel Canning shot dead, Captain Gordon mortally wounded. The Prince of Orange lost his left arm. (The sacred box containing it can still be seen privately in a Netherlands museum.) To his officers in general Wellington spoke with an echo of Shakespeare's Henry V. It was hard pounding and they must see who could pound the longest: 'We must not be beaten – what will they say in England.'

7–9 p.m.

A royalist deserter informed Wellington that Napoleon's Imperial Guard were coming. The excitement was intense as Bonaparte led out his 'Immortelles' himself, Grenadiers, Chasseurs of the Middle Guard – a total of

15,000 men. He handed the Grenadiers over to Ney at La Haye Sainte and dealt with an alarming rumour that Prussian troops had been seen with his usual magic. Waving his wand, he changed 'The Prussians are coming' into an announcement that French reinforcements were arriving – 'Voilà Grouchy!' A lie never came amiss. And so they marched on joyfully through the smoke and the mud, waving at each discharge like corn in the wind, towards Death the reaper.

The Duke had his infantry lying down behind the crest. His Guards had watched the French battalions snaking across the valley like some primeval reptile. Now it was the long blue overcoats of the dreaded *Garde*, packed close together, and already a bloody target for the Allied gunners, who were coming at them. It was Wellington himself who galloped to give General Maitland the signal: 'Now Maitland, now is your time. Stand up Guards!'*

The Duke had already rallied two battalions of very youthful Brunswickers and other units showing signs of confusion were stabilised when Maitland's Guards finally made their spectacular entry into the dreadful drama. At the command 'Stand up!', 1,500 men sprang to their feet as if out of the earth. Many were indeed to

---

* That Wellington launched his early nineteenth-century Guards in language used by the rank-and-file a century later – 'Up Guards and at 'em' – cannot be accepted. It is a tradition not based on evidence.)

return to the earth all too soon, but meanwhile their tactical innovations enabled them to bring their total fire-power to bear on the enemy, now only twenty yards away. For a moment the startled *Garde* gaped at the apparition but came on steadily, marching on to the bayonets, a steel wall from which there was no escape – except by flight. And this was precisely what they chose. So tightly packed that they could not deploy to return the murderous fire, they stood and were massacred until, inevitably, the long blue overcoats began to waver. Their supporters, raked with violent fire by Colbourne's 52nd Foot, suddenly set up a cry of anguish more dreadful than anything their own sufferings could evoke. The bravest of the brave were running away. The 'Immortelles' were mortal: 'La Garde recule!'

Wellington as usual seemed to be everywhere at once on the battlefield, the spirit of urgency. When a group of soldiers recognised him and began to cheer, as they always did, he would say: 'No cheering my lads, but forward and complete your victory!' When his remaining aides-de-camp begged him to expose himself less, the reply was: 'So I will, when we have driven those fellows off.' And when the gallant Colbourne asked anxiously if he had brought the 52nd too far forward, he got the urgent reply: 'Well done, Colbourne! Well done! Go on, never mind, *go* on, *go* on. Don't give them time to rally. They won't stand.'

Napoleon's army was shaken, not routed. There was still, at 7.30 p.m., half-an-hour of daylight left.

Wellington's force was down to 35,000 men, all of them trusty and determined. So now it was up to the Prussians and Blücher's promise. For the hundredth time Wellington swept the eastern hills with his telescope. What he saw made him call an aide-de-camp and send him spurring down the Highlanders' rear: 'The day is our own! The Prussians have arrived!' He had seen that the enemy on their extreme right were caught in a cross-fire.

Some of those around the Duke advised only a limited response at first to this new, exciting situation. The Duke knew better: 'Oh, dammit', he shouted as he tore off his hat and waved it three times towards the French, 'In for a penny, in for a pound!' In a whirl of relief and joy, his men responded to the three waves with three mighty cheers and the foremost regiment, led by Sir Hussey Vivian's and Sir John Ormsby Vandeleur's light cavalry, swooped into the valley.

One of the last French cannon shots to rake the fields below La Haye Sainte skimmed over Copenhagen's neck and smashed into Uxbridge's right knee. 'By God! I've lost my leg!'

'Have you, by God?' replied Wellington, as he supported the heroic Uxbridge until he was helped down and carried away. There were many occasions on the battlefield when Napoleon's adoption and Wellington's earlier rejection of a brilliant innovation – the ambulance – showed Napoleon in the lead. Uxbridge's leg, however, became one of the heroes of Waterloo and was buried there in a little garden of remembrance.

Meanwhile, Sir Hussey Vivian called on his hussars, 'Follow me!' to which they roared back, 'To hell!' And to hell it was, for the fetlocks of their horses were terribly wounded by the bayonets sticking up all over the field. The French in La Haye Sainte and the gravel-pit were driven out by the Highlanders, yelling like a 'legion of demons' as they mingled triumphantly with the first Prussians to reach the Brussels road. Well-meant attempts to protect the Duke's 'precious life' were again made and repudiated: 'The battle's won; my life's of no consequence now', he answered, using the opposite reason from the one he had given earlier for staying at his post.

The French cries of anguish, most memorable in history, were now beginning to accumulate. First 'La Garde recule'; then, when the Prussians appeared instead of Grouchy, 'Nous sommes trahis' – 'We are betrayed'; followed by 'Sauve qui peut' – 'Every man for himself'. Fear of treachery has been described as the 'heart-cry of Napoleon's Hundred'. Yet despite all the horror and misery of the French on the evening of 18 June 1815, the Allies could not but be impressed by the final vision of a fragment of the old *Garde* stalking majestically off the field. No treachery. No panic. Napoleon himself made an escape from the scene of the disaster in his elegant dark blue carriage with bright red wheels. Before the oncoming Prussians could capture the carriage with its human treasure inside, he had leapt onto a horse, reaching his headquarters at Charleroi at 5 o'clock next morning in safety. The rest of the coach's treasure fell into Prussian hands: a million francs worth of diamonds and a cake of Windsor soap – the nearest Bonaparte was to get to a second Norman Conquest. They presented the carriage itself to England's Prince Regent. (It went up in flames in 1925.)

While Napoleon shared in his army's shameful new battle cry – 'Every man for himself' – the Duke and Blücher were staking out their shared claim to victory. It was 9 p.m. and nearly dark: the scene was near La Belle-Alliance on the Brussels road. Blücher rode forward to greet his 'liebe Kamerad' in what were, according to Wellington, the only French words that the Prussian knew – 'Quelle affaire'. War was a little mad, just like Blücher, for in war two Allies could converse together only in the language of the common enemy.

But to Wellington the field of battle came to mean something worse than a vein of dottiness. Perhaps this is the moment to look ahead at the Duke's final reaction to war. If war was a little mad, battles were ultimately bad, although, of course, there was heroism on the battlefield, both solemn and light-hearted. As Wellington rode slowly back to his inn at Waterloo, he saw the piles of dead and the occasional robber looking more ghastly than ever in the moonlight. He was shocked by the gaps at his supper-table, the enormity of the losses – Allies to French. He was no longer a 'beau' that night as he lay down to sleep unwashed and still in his battle clothes. When they read him the lists of casualties next morning, the dust and grime was still on his cheeks, to be furrowed by tears. His favourite aide-de-camp, young Alexander Gordon had been laid in the Duke's bed and died there that night. Young Fitzroy Somerset was heroic, too, though he played for a laugh when the surgeons amputated his smashed arm, shouting: 'Hi, don't throw it away, I want my ring!' (It was the wedding ring he had worn at his marriage to Emily, Wellington's niece.)

The battle could be described in language that was equally sincere whether highly coloured or quietly restrained. Wellington's famous Waterloo Despatch avoided individual names. The Horse Artillery were not mentioned by name, nor any of the Hussar regiments, nor Colborne and his victorious 52nd. A reference to bravery found its way into the text only once as did steadiness and glory, but there were four mentions of distinguished or highly distinguished conduct and five of gallantry or the utmost gallantry. At home, every sentence of the statement was scrutinised for praise or neglect of individuals or regiments, and the Duke's sparing hand certainly had an effect on his popularity. Though Wellington continued to stand for an almost classical restraint in all things, his final judgement on the Waterloo Despatch was critical: 'I should have given more praise.' This admission was revealed many years after the hero's death by Sir Winston Churchill who reported it as the aged Duke's response when asked by a friend whether, if he had his life over again, there was anything he could have done better. But Wellington would never have agreed with Churchill's view that only in the ultimate test of battle could man give of his very best. Wellington's basic principle was: 'There was glory enough for all.'

Wellington's own view on Waterloo was expressed to four individuals: Dr Hume, Creevey the writer, Lady Shelley and young Lady Salisbury. The first revelation took place on the morning after the battle. Wellington's doctor, John Hume, had just read him the casualty list. 'Well, thank God I don't know what it is to lose a battle', he said: 'but certainly nothing could be more painful than to gain one, with the loss of so many of one's friends.' A little later Creevey, when passing under the Duke's window and still confused by contradictory Brussels reports, called out: 'What's the news?' The Duke summoned him: 'Why, I think we have done for 'em this time', and then called Creevey up. 'It has been a dammed serious business. Blücher and I have lost 30,000 men. It has been a dammed nice thing – the nearest run thing you ever saw in your life.' (The corrected figures were between 22,000 and 23,000.) Finally, he burst out to Creevey: 'By God! I don't think it would have done if I had not been there.' Later, he gave credit to that most perfect of instruments, the British infantry; and also, in a note to Lady Frances Wedderburn-Webster, to his oldest of supporters, the finger of Providence. 'The finger of Providence was upon me and I escaped unhurt.' Within a few weeks of Waterloo he was telling Lady Shelley: 'I hope to God that I have fought my last battle. It is a bad thing to be always fighting.'

But was it a bad thing to be henceforth and for always a national hero? This was Wellington's new position. He had left civilian life for military life in 1808. Now he had to start again – at the top. Not any easy proposition. His young friend Lady Salisbury attempted more than once to discover how he would face and tackle the difficulties. In 1836 she tried in vain to explore the sensations of personal glory he must have felt on the morning after Waterloo. 'I cannot conceive', she challenged, 'how it was that you did not think how infinitely you had raised your name above every other.' In other words, how could a hero not feel heroic? 'That is a feeling of vanity', he replied. 'One's first thought is for the public service.' But she would not let go. Surely there must be a satisfaction in always doing his job better than anyone else could? A feeling of superiority? He conceded that point; but after the war was over, what was the great general? Carpenters, shoemakers and farmers did their own job better than he could. She failed utterly to make him speak with the tongue of a hero. When they had welcomed him at Cádiz as the hero of the Peninsular War, he had felt the need of always having someone behind him to remind him that 'I am but a man.'

NINE

WESTMINSTER
WARRIORS

After Waterloo – what? Great wars usher in periods of great reform in civil life. After the 1914–18 conflict came at last the definitive advance in the role of women. After the Napoleonic Wars, Wellington would be called upon to advance the religious and political rights of the ordinary male. Napoleon had been dead eight years when the Duke introduced Catholic emancipation in 1829.*

It was many months after the great battle before the Prince of Waterloo was ready to leave Paris, with its parties and problems. His sad little Duchess Kitty joined him there after four months, but her presence in no way

---

* Sadly for Napoleon, the example he had set of escaping from Elba, meant that his enemies' second choice for him was St Helena in 1815, from which he could escape only by death. The news of his death in 1821 was announced to George IV with the words: 'Sir, your greatest enemy is dead.' To which the King replied, 'Is she, by God?' thinking they were referring to the demise of his detested wife Caroline.

mitigated the ebullience of his favourite ladies, including Mrs Arbuthnot, Lady Shelley, the Ladies Charlotte Greville, Frances Wedderburn-Webster and Caroline Lamb – with four classy courtesans thrown in. Lady Shelley, in her adoration of the great man, studied every detail of his behaviour. Why did his face stiffen when his soldiers cheered him? If you let them cheer today, they might hiss tomorrow: 'However, I cannot always prevent my fellows from giving me a hurrah!'

As for the problems, the main ones concerned accepting the French surrender with as much humanity as possible. The British Army, as always since 1808, was forbidden to pillage or destroy; England, unlike Prussia, had never been ravaged by Bonaparte and there was no excuse for revenge. The Duke also ran into difficulties indulging his pleasure in giving pretty women advice, but more dangerous were the problems presented by the French 'Ultras', whose animosity towards the Duke did not stop at violence, once, indeed, resulting in an attempt on his life.

Wellington returned from Paris to his own island, loaded with honours and with two stately homes in which to enjoy them – Apsley House and Stratfield Saye. Created Prince of Waterloo, he was presented with a diamond sword by Tsar Alexander, under the title of Conqueror of Waterloo – just so that there need never be any doubt about who had won. (Unfortunately, there was doubt. By the end of 1815 the Prince of Orange and the Prussians were each claiming victory, and in 2000 a German wrote to the English press still claiming it.)

The lovely estate of Stratfield Saye was waiting for him in Hampshire. Kitty also felt happy there for the little bedroom and sitting-room into which she moved were reassuringly like her old day nursery at Pakenham Hall, the family home in Ireland. Stratfield Saye was a gift to the national hero. Wellington bought Apsley House at Hyde Park Corner to be his family's town house. It was to be known as Number One, London.

At last the time had come for the Prince of Waterloo to shine again as the 'Duke' in England. In 1818 he moved into Apsley House, along with his Duchess, their two sons, Arthur and Charles, and the Duke's military cook, Thornton. Thornton, however, cooked for Kitty as if he were still feeding an army in the Peninsula or France, or even that last ghostly supper at Waterloo where so many places were laid and so few survived to eat; Thornton was finally taken on elsewhere in a position more appropriate to his talents. And the nation's hero himself? Home for him was now to be an England at peace, but not at rest, victorious, but not without enemies, with a battlefield at Westminster, if not in Flanders.

It had been rumoured in the press that when the occupation of France ended and the Duke returned home in 1818, he would join Lord Liverpool's Tory government. Many of the Duke's friends refused to believe it, especially General Alava, a close friend and Spanish Liberal. The Duke a politician? The Duke a party politician? The Great Duke a Tory party politician? No, no, no to all three. Yet it was true – although on the Duke's own terms. He became Lord Liverpool's Master-General of the Ordnance – without being necessarily bound to the fate of the Tory party. Tories might come and Tories might go, the Duke went on for ever. It was his vocation to save the country.

Unhappily 1818 was the start of a bad period for British political life, haunted as it was by three spectres: cash, Catholics and corn.

Cash in short supply and rampant poverty led to the terrible event known as Peterloo, when Britain's mighty arm, instead of being used to right wrongs as at Waterloo was twisted into a police cudgel to smash the pacific demonstrations of the poor in St Peter's Fields, Manchester on 16 August 1819. As a member of a government that backed the unpopular King against the mob's favourite, Queen Caroline, the Duke shared the Cabinet's troubles. A contemporary print shows him galloping into Parliament Square through a crowd of bystanders who are greeting the hero of Waterloo with hisses. Worse still, a battalion of Guards showed their devotion to Caroline and mutinied. But at least this disgrace was responsible for one of the best innovations of the early nineteenth century: the Duke wrote a memorandum recommending the introduction of an independent police force. Eight years later (1828), this resulted in the creation, under Wellington as Prime Minister and Sir Robert Peel as Home Secretary, of

London's first 'bobbies' or 'Peelites' – the indispensable police force.

It seemed in these first years after Waterloo that the Duke was likely to manage the nation's domestic life better than his own. He and Kitty had always been mismatched. Now her constant demands for a larger allowance were met by roughly expressed refusals. He was under the impression that it all went on beggars she could not resist and so gave him – the Great Duke – a bad name for not paying his household bills. In fact, the first part of his accusation may have been true; but the Duke had forgotten her immense charitable work for children, some of whom were his own relations whom she helped or even adopted when their families failed them. Her greatest pleasure in life was the strong bond between herself and their two sons, Arthur, now Lord Douro, and the younger, now Lord Charles Wellesley.

Within less than two decades after Waterloo, the Duke's and the nation's domestic crises had erupted; in fact, erupted more than once, so that the hero's career was to follow a new direction and take on a new atmosphere yet again.

To deal with his married life first, we must look forward to the year 1831 and the month of January. Kitty lay in a spacious ground-floor room of Apsley House, on a high white bed-sofa from which she could see and revel in her husband's trophies: porcelain, silver and above all the golden shield of Achilles. The Duke had never left her side during her illness, but today she had a visitor from Ireland, her old friend Maria Edgeworth, the famous novelist. Maria hoped Kitty would not outlive the Iron Duke's new tenderness. The wish, however uncharitably expressed, was to be granted. Maria believed the small waxen figure was dying of cancer; others thought it was cholera. The end came on 24 April 1831. The Duke's praises had been on her lips as she lay on her deathbed. All these trophies and these tributes to his greatness – they were all 'pure' no trace of 'corruption anywhere'. Not even of the great Duke of Marlborough could the same be said. Once as he sat at her bedside, she felt up his sleeve to find out if he was still wearing an armlet she had given him long ago. Yes, it was there. And always had been, as he told a friend afterwards, had she cared to look. She was buried in the family vault at Stratfield Saye.*

Death had also cleared the nation's political stage to some purpose. With the death of the commander-in-chief of the British Army, the Duke of York on 5 January 1827, Death made sure of a remarkable harvest for many days to come. At that period a royal death meant a funeral in St George's Chapel, Windsor, by night, with nothing to prevent the icy damp rising in winter from the royal flagstones. After the Duke of York's burial on

---

* Later in the nineteenth century, Sir Robert Peel's daughter was to marry the Earl of Jersey, and their daughter Mary was to marry Thomas, Earl of Longford. Thus the author of the present brief biography has married into a family in which Wellesleys, Peels and Pakenhams are all distantly related.

20 January Death the reaper made sure of two bishops, five footmen and several soldiers; two leading politicians, George Canning and William Huskisson, caught chills from which they never completely recovered. Wellington fell ill on his way home, but though prostrated for a time, the hero of many mountainous battlefields did not succumb. Lord Liverpool, the Prime Minister, himself already too ill to attend a nocturnal funeral, died on 17 February of a stroke. And on 9 April, Canning, the Foreign Secretary, became the new Tory Prime Minister.

Canning was a man of ideas. To him Europe owed the celebrated idea of 'calling in the New World to restore the balance of the old'. As a progressive Tory, at this time absorbed in two subjects for reform – Catholic emancipation and corn – Canning was anathema to the high Tories, of whom Wellington was one. When Canning invited the Duke to join his new Cabinet, the Duke not only refused but also resigned the post of commander-in-chief of the British army, despite the fact that he had always said the army was non-party political. To make matters worse, his Tory colleague Sir Robert Peel advised him to stand up in Parliament and defend his resignation from the Cabinet, since there were various malicious rumours that he had wanted to be Prime Minister himself. Wellington accordingly addressed the House of Lords in words that were to be less than no use to his future career – indeed they might well have proved fatal. Disclaiming any desire or suitability for the premiership, he added by way of punch-line: 'My lords, I should have been worse than mad if I had thought of such a thing.' Surely, if every soldier carried a field marshal's baton in his knapsack, as Napoleon said, every politician was right to expect a PM's commission in his mail – some day. Wellington himself had made it more than likely that the commission would never be his.

However, Death again took a bony hand in all their fates. Canning's popularity was as strong as his health was weak. He skilfully postponed the unpopular subject of Catholic rights and worked on a new law to reform the duties on imported corn so that bread might be cheaper in those days of hunger. Wellington and the anti-Canningites opposed a new Corn Bill with such vigour that it was suggested that public admiration for the Wellington boot would soon change into loathing for the Wellington loaf – a loaf that the poor, whether English or Irish, could never afford. Suddenly, on 3 August, Wellington heard Canning had been taken desperately ill. By 8 August 1827, exactly 100 days after he first faced Parliament as Prime Minister, Canning was dead; some said broken down by the jibes of the Opposition leader, Lord Grey. The Canningites managed to survive under the premiership of Lord Goderich, liberal-minded but tearful ever since the loss of his eleven-year-old daughter. 'Blubbering idiot', muttered the King as tears fell on the hand that the new Prime Minister kissed.

Two months later the naval victory of Navarino, when Admiral Codrington sent the Turkish fleet to the bottom of the sea, caused worse than blubbering. The Whigs found it more glorious than anything since Byron's death for Greece and Freedom. The government, reported Mrs Arbuthnot, were 'frightened to death'. The King gave Codrington the ribbon (Bath) but said he deserved the rope. Goderich dissolved in tears and dissolved the government, too. At 9 a.m. on 9 January 1828, the Lord Chancellor, Lord Lyndhurst, called at Apsley House and swept Wellington away to Windsor where King George IV appointed him Prime Minister.

The King normally wrote to his new premier as 'My dear Friend' or 'My dear Arthur', occasionally referring to him as 'King Arthur' when he thought he had got too big for his Wellington boots. At fifty-nine, the Duke's speech was clear and his blue-grey eyes as bright as ever. His hair still sprung up from his broad forehead, his nose was long and so was his chin. Two years before she herself died, Kitty was impressed by his vitality. Sometimes it was his sharpness that impressed the world most. An official in Pall Mall once mistook him for the secretary of the Royal Academy. 'Mr Jones, I believe', he said blandly. 'If you believe that, you'll believe anything', was the cutting reply.

Vitality was indeed necessary for the task in hand – the one that Canning had postponed and Goderich had not had a chance to reach – Catholic emancipation. Ever since the Act of Union, Ireland had had no Parliament of its own in Dublin. Irishmen – Catholics and Protestants alike – could vote in 1828 for their representatives at

Westminster. The voters could be Catholics but they could not vote *for* Catholics. If an Irish Catholic chose to stand for Parliament and was elected, he could not take his seat. This was the result of religious prejudice that was soon to make Ireland ungovernable, for its population was largely Catholic.

Wellington was a specialist in law and order. He had trained armies in the arts of law and order; he had repudiated the barbarism of suppression by violence. How could he respond to the challenging problems of the island of his birth? In any case they could not be solved by Wellington as commander-in-chief of the army, a post which he had long since resumed at the King's invitation, for his new political colleagues had insisted that he should again resign it. (According to his own words, being the commander-in-chief was incompatible with being Prime Minister.)

The fight for and against Catholic emancipation (or Relief, as it was also called) began in the first few months of the Duke's premiership. In April 1828 he had as usual expressed his opposition to it. In June the bill, introduced yet again, passed the Commons by a mere six votes and was rejected by Wellington in the Lords with the usual firmness. Had he not already said the last word on the subject in a speech on 24 April? – '. . . there is no person in this House whose feelings are more decided than mine are with regard to the subject of Roman Catholic claims; and until I see a great change in that quarter, I certainly shall oppose it.' In fact the great 'change' was already on the way.

A by-election was due in Ireland's County Clare in July. On nomination day, 30 June, the Catholic nationalist leader, Daniel O'Connell presented himself at Ennis, Clare's county town, as a candidate, for though the law forbade a Catholic to *sit* in Parliament it did not forbid a Catholic to *stand*. Polling began on 1 July, with vast orderly processions carrying green banners, green branches, green shamrocks and Daniel O'Connell marching to the polls. The great Dan was the victor by 2,057 votes to 982. Ireland – and, for that matter, England too – would never be the same again. Indeed, the Duke was caught in something like a vice between the English House of Commons and the Irish voters. Worn out and exhausted, he paced up and down Birdcage Walk with Mrs Harriet Arbuthnot as a companion. Suddenly she heard her hero say: 'This state of things cannot be allowed to continue.' It was the moment when the Duke was converted to Catholic emancipation.

Though the Duke had voted so often in Parliament against the Catholic cause, his views were in fact curiously moderate for one with his reputation. He believed it to be perfectly natural that Irish Catholics should want the same rights as Protestants. The only special need in the case of Catholic emancipation was for 'safeguards'.

Sir Robert Peel was another matter. He felt totally unable at first to support the Prime Minister in working out a Catholic emancipation bill. Yet Peel's support was essential. He was the Duke's right-hand man, as well as being his powerful Home Secretary. After much painful argument, Peel was won round, though on the impossible condition that the Duke accepted his resignation after the bill was safely through.

After much heart-burning the King was persuaded to give the Cabinet permission to work on their Irish bill, the date now being January 1829. But under pressure from his most loved and feared brother, the reactionary Duke of Cumberland, the King received Wellington with hysterical animosity on 25 February, hurling after him one of his favourite epigrams: 'Arthur is king of England, O'Connell king of Ireland – and I suppose I am Dean of Windsor.' The Duke had left out Cumberland, the Lord of Misrule.

Wellington, having discovered a Cumberland plot to make the royal household vote against the government, again tackled His Majesty, who in March gave his friend Arthur (arm round his neck at parting) authority to make the household vote straight and their corrupter return to Germany. All done in a flood of tears. But the King had still not humiliated himself or his office enough. On 4 March he summoned Wellington, Peel and Lyndhurst to Windsor and retracted his permission for the bill. The dauntless three resigned on the spot and the King, foreseeing his country without government sent a messenger galloping along the Windsor–London road to find Wellington and cancel His Majesty's latest nonsense.

Peel's brilliant oratory in support of the bill fanned the Protestant fanatics into theatrical opposition, as when Sir Charles Wetherell, the Protestant Attorney-General managed to undo his braces while orating so that his waistcoat rode up and his breeches fell down in defence of the Protestant cause. Wellington's only rest came between 7 and 12 March when an appalling cold caused him to be bled and – horror of horrors – to describe himself as 'a sick man'. One imaginative Protestant, Lord Winchilsea, saw the bill as Wellington's plot to deliver Protestant England, including Parliament and King's College, into the hands of the Pope. With equal lack of good sense the enraged Duke challenged Winchilsea to a duel on Battersea Fields. Fortunately no damage was done, for duelling was illegal in 1829.

On 10 April 1829 Wellington moved the third reading of the bill. It was carried by a majority of 104: 213 votes to 109. Wellington's cheerful reaction was to be short-lived. He greeted Lord Dungannon most enthusiastically after the vote: 'Well, I said I would do it, and I have done it handsomely.' But by 13 April, the day when royal assent was given, he was seen leaving the chamber with a pale face and his cloak drawn tight around him. Harriet Arbuthnot probably interpreted the gesture correctly, for she said he needed to draw the Tories closely round him once again. But such was the first glow of national gratitude for his non-party achievement that some felt his present glory outshone even Waterloo.

The next national glow was in response to Peel's invention of the police. Two reforms in one year: could it last? Balancing the nation's satisfaction was the increasing hostility of the royal brothers, King George and Duke Ernest. Wellington soon believed that the growing weakness of his government was ultimately due to the King, who would in due course dismiss him as Prime Minister. 'I don't believe the King', said Mrs Arbuthnot stoutly. Her idol had recovered his health, and his face, for months pale and drawn, was again quite full and florid. By September, in fact, the Duke was well enough to enjoy his battle with the King. But another word even more potent than 'Catholic' had begun to take over the political discussion – 'Distress'.

The relief of distress had taken over from Catholic relief as the political heart-cry of the times. The poverty that showed itself at the end of the Napoleonic Wars had not been exorcised by Peterloo or any other demonstration. Sixteen million people now lived in Britain and of these a shocking number could be called starving. The enclosure of common land was partly responsible for driving more and more country folk into the city ant-heaps. (It is to Wellington's credit that he refused to enclose a common near Stratfield Saye as recommended by his agent.) But a deadlier factor was the high duty on imported corn, which in turn put their staple diet – bread – beyond the purses of the poor.

The Duke recognised that discontent was part of the 'spirit of the times' but he mistook its cause for the receding groundswell of Catholic relief, instead of seeing it as a sign of oncoming storms. He himself felt the need of 'relief'. His situation seemed to be the same as when he commanded the army: nothing worked unless he gave his whole mind and experience to it. Yet he longed to quit office. Before he became Prime Minister he had no dispute or differences with anybody – except 'the scum of the earth'. Today, except for Clarence, none of the royal family would speak to him. How could he paper over the various cracks? In the old days there was patronage. But it had been his own policy to abolish every sinecure as it fell in. 'I should be more than Man if I did not feel the Misery of my position.' Yet it was he who had said: 'I am but a Man.' Even the great Hoby, maker of his 'Wellington boots', had failed him. The last pair had made him lame.

With so many things going awry Wellington must have felt it right that he should be made George IV's executor when he died on 26 June 1830. As Wellington saw it, this enabled him to protect the country as a whole, as well as the royal family, from the scandalous revelations that might otherwise have occurred. For instance, the Duke of Cumberland, George IV's brother, 'more than once attempted to violate' the person of his sister Princess Sophia; through Wellington this was kept dark for 140 years. Again, a box of letters was brought to Wellington in 1835 which would have delighted the 'Radical Revolutionaries', as he called them. They were written between George and Caroline, Prince and Princess of Wales. He burnt them.

Meanwhile, he had written a letter in 1830 to Peel, resigning his office of Prime Minister in favour of Peel himself. The letter was written but never sent. How could

Wellington bring himself to install that strange, austere man, full of odd ideas of reform, as the country's chief bastion against a possible wave of radical revolutionaries? Pulling back from this decision was one of the big mistakes of Wellington's life and it left him to face an impending crisis in the worst possible circumstances.

The death of George IV in 1830 demanded a general election and the reign of William IV, formerly Duke of Clarence, began in 1830 with another victory for the Tories and Wellington, still Prime Minister. Within three months, however, revolution abroad and demands for parliamentary reform at home drove Wellington into the most unexpected and immoderate speech of his life. Across the Channel, Charles X, the King of France, was overthrown and replaced by Louis-Philippe, who styled himself King of the French. In England, distress among the agricultural labourers led to machine-breaking in Kent and Sussex, where the threshing machines snatched away the people's work just when winter was coming and they needed it.

Wellington was not impressed by the efforts made to frighten him and the gentlemen of Kent: hay-ricks burning with a strange blue flame, Captain Swing, who was supposed to ride around the countryside wreaking vengeance but in fact was nothing but a name. Lord Camden, a Kent landowner who was terrified out of his wits, implored Wellington to place reformers in his Parliament before worse disasters befell. The Duke's characteristic reaction to Camden was: 'I am more afraid of terror than I am of anything else.'

It might have been supposed that the Duke would favour the development of the Iron Horse as a counterbalance to Captain Swing and other wild men of the downs. The railways were coming along fast in the 1830s, with locomotives travelling at between twelve and thirty miles a hour. But the Duke was unimpressed, particularly after a train killed his supporter Huskisson. The Duke regarded the train as having butted in just as the horse-drawn coach had reached perfection.

On 2 November 1830 he made a great speech opposing parliamentary reform, such as the abolition of rotten boroughs and the widening of the franchise. At each stage of the speech Wellington worked himself into an unusual fury, pushing himself further and further in the direction of anti-reform. But could he really be against reform itself, as well as against the radical revolutionaries and wild men who often promoted it, men whom in the old days he would cheerfully have called the scum of the earth? He spoke the answer loud and clear: 'I shall therefore at all times and under all circumstances oppose it.'

It was not as if the reformers who were actually in Parliament had tried to drive the debate to extremes. True, some radicals, like Henry Brougham MP, were clamouring for annual elections, universal suffrage and the secret ballot. But Lord Grey, leader of the Whig (or Liberal) Opposition, expressed moderate views, admiration for the Duke and no support for the extreme radicals. Nevertheless, Wellington was set on driving himself further. The British system of parliamentary voting was the best in the world, he declared, and it would be impossible to equal, much less to surpass, its perfections. Its special excellence depended on its being heavily weighted in favour of the landed proprietor. And not only was he not prepared to bring forward any measures of reform himself, 'but . . . I shall always feel it my duty to resist such measures when proposed by others'.

As he sat down, the long, gloomy face of Lord Aberdeen, his Foreign Secretary, looked gloomier than ever. The House could scarcely believe what it had been hearing. The funds fell; there were rumours in the city of a foreign conspiracy. The truth was that Wellington was a natural military hero but not a born politician. He was like a doctor with no gift for diagnosis. He and a friend used to play a game together when driving about the country in an open carriage: 'What's on the other side of the Hill?' Wellington was much better than his friend Croker at guessing correctly the military terrain that lay just round the corner and acting accordingly. But he was less good at predicting the political terrain. The Duke got his first death threat in a note from Captain Swing on 8 November.

The greatest test was to come in mid-November 1830. Harriet Arbuthnot wrote in her journal on the 15th that Peel could not go on any longer in the Commons alone. On that very morning a great wave of rebellion swept through the House and the Ultra-Tories, cheered by the Whigs, defeated the government. Peel looked radiant to see the end of his purgatory in sight. A note was carried to the Duke who was entertaining the Prince of Orange to dinner in the Waterloo Chamber at Apsley House. Passing the note to Mrs Arbuthnot, he went down to the House. It was agreed that the Duke must resign next morning. Peel kept smiling.

To fall from power only three months after winning an election was indeed most extraordinary, but the British people had become absolutely determined that something radical should happen. For his part, the Duke had told his friend Colin Campbell that he expected to serve his country in the army but if the country wanted him for minister he would do what he could. Five years after his fall he was telling Lady Salisbury how much better it was to be served by officers than by Cabinet ministers. ('I say to one, "Go", and he goes, and to another, "Come", and he comes.') The Wellington method with the army had a biblical ring about it, though it was, if possible, even more autocratic. He described how he laid his plan, in each case, before his officers and it was carried out 'without any more words'. That may have been good enough for a dear old half-tipsy, blind general like Erskine. What about Peel? Fortunately, when he was in the army the charm of Arthur's manner more than balanced the firmness of his voice.

There has always been a tendency to regard the Duke as a moderniser *malgre lui* — a natural reactionary who was forced to learn new tricks against his will. This is a mistake. If one needs a label for him, it is better to avoid both 'reactionary' and 'reformer' and to use a still more general word like 'pragmatist'. Arthur had always wanted things to work. If the government of Ireland would not work properly without Catholic relief, then the Catholics must be relieved of their present burden – living in communities without full citizenship. If London as a city needed its own new police, then the innovator Peel must be able to give it. But even pragmatists do not always agree with change. There was one at least who did not believe the constitution would work better after an extension of the franchise or that the country as a whole would be better off with cheaper bread. That man was Wellington.

After a spell at Stratfield Saye the Duke was beginning to look better, but not so Harriet Arbuthnot. She left her first journal entry for 1831 unfinished, with a stranded '&', as if to symbolise her disenchantment with Whig dreams.

The Great Reform Bill was introduced by Lord John Russell in the Commons and Lord Grey, the new Prime Minister, in the Lords, to whom Wellington, in a short, two or three minute speech of doom prophesied the most appalling future: 'from the period of the adoption of that measure will date the downfall of the Constitution'. Though Wellington emphasised that he himself had no personal interests involved in the destruction of rotten boroughs, the plan was to abolish sixty completely and partially disfranchise a further forty – all owned by somebody like the notorious Duke of Newcastle, who once dared to say the unforgettable words: 'I shall do what I like with my own.'

There was an exciting scene between the Palace and Westminster. King William IV jibbed at the demand that he should dissolve Parliament, scribbling on a slip of paper: 'I consider Dissolution Tantamount to Revolution'. But when he heard that a Tory peer intended to thwart his royal right to dissolve, he had the crown rushed from the Tower, his robes from Sir William Beechey's studio, and his Master of Horse from a late breakfast in order to escort his royal coach to Parliament. Lord Albemarle gasped and asked if there were a revolution: '. . . there will be, if you stay to finish your breakfast'. Parliament was dissolved. Peel's auburn hair blazed like Marshal Ney's at Waterloo as he opposed the triumphant Whigs; like Ney, Peel was defeated. There was no Wellington to stand in his place, for Kitty was dying. The end came on 24 April 1831, two days after the King dissolved the last truly Tory, unreformed Parliament. The rout of the Tories followed, in an election defeat of 140 votes. There followed a ludicrous exposure of Wellington's 'perfect' system on 8 October. His troops in the House of Lords voted down the Reform Bill by a thumping majority of 41 votes. Progress – or indeed any movement – under this 'perfection' was impossible.

But the Duke was too good a soldier not to know the answer. After several bold attempts to rescue His Majesty from the Whigs by again becoming Tory Minister himself (Peel would not play, being brilliant but timid), the Duke came to a dramatic decision: he must retreat into a political Lines of Torres Vedras, within which the Tory creed would lie safe and ultimately might emerge stronger than ever. So he fought the May Days of 1832.

On 7 May the third attempt to get the Reform Bill through the House of Lords was defeated. On that same Monday, 150,000 members of the Birmingham Union sang their hymn: 'We will, we will, *we will be free*'. The crisis deepened. On 8 May, Lord Grey demanded of the King the creation of at least fifty peers to outvote the Tory Opposition in the Lords but on the 9th William refused. Grey resigned and William commissioned Wellington to bring in the reforms to which the country was entitled. There was heavy enrolment in the political unions. On 10 May, with quixotic loyalty to the crown, Wellington agreed. Not so Peel, who refused any office. The Stock Exchange closed and notices appeared in house windows: 'No taxes paid here till the Reform Bill is passed'. By the 11th plans were being laid in the radical home of Francis Place to resist Wellington and on the 12th barricades were planned for Birmingham and Manchester. On 13 May the Scots Greys were ordered to rough-sharpen their sabres and the following day wild rumours circulated that Wellington was to be assassinated on the way to Parliament. His niece begged him to go in her carriage, incognito: 'I could no more go . . . in your carriage,' he replied, 'than I could crawl . . . [on] all fours.' Grey was recalled to Windsor on the 15th, the Duke having informed William there was no support in the

Commons. Parliament was adjourned. On 17 May came the warning that unless His Majesty promised to create peers, there was a risk of revolution.

At this point, the Duke rescued William from his dilemma by promising to retreat rather than drive the King to extremes. But all he would reveal in the Lords of his promise were a few moving words: 'If I had been capable of refusing my assistance to His Majesty, I do not think, my Lords, that I could have shown my face in the streets for shame.' He did not reveal that this was in fact his farewell speech, but the House was deeply stirred.

On 18 May the *Morning Chronicle* talked of 'the eve of the barricades'; but the King gave his written guarantee to create peers if necessary and the Duke and a hundred other Tories promised to abstain from the vote on Reform. Earl Grey announced victory – the Duke had had a share in it – and on 4 June 1832, the bill was read a third time, and was passed by 106 votes to 22.

Again drawing inspiration from his military past, Wellington knew that there was a time for advance and a time for retreat. He received a letter from his friend Croker, who said he could not serve and would not stand for the new reformed House of Commons. That was not Wellington's creed. He had never found it impossible to serve.

There was a brief but fervent reaction in the Duke's favour after the windows of Apsley House had been smashed by the mob in 1831. But he sensed that public opinion was hostile to him and felt himself banished like

Napoleon to an Elba of his own. The death of Kitty had contributed to his feelings of gloom.

In the new election the Whigs won 320 seats and the Conservatives only 150. Asked what the Duke thought of the remodelled Parliament as he surveyed the new MPs from the Peers' Gallery, he replied: 'I have never seen so many bad hats in my life.' Despite this basic distrust he decided that the Conservatives must not harass Grey's government, nor must they set out to encourage any political upheaval in the country. Any full-scale attack on the government must be avoided except on 'occasions of great importance'. When the Whigs sought to reform the Irish Protestant Church with the Irish Church Bill of 1833, Wellington felt that this was the moment to sharpen his sabre. He denounced the bill on 11 July, but when the Ultra-Tories became overexcited and threatened mutiny in the Lords, he decided to continue with the policy of pricking rather than puncturing the Whigs. Despite his own revulsion at the possibility of a Catholic bishop occupying a Protestant bishop's palace and even using the 'very furniture', he could not vote against the bill. Instead he abstained, much to the rage of the Ultras. The bill was saved. He had managed to prevent the head-on collision between the Lords and the Commons that the King dreaded above all.

The Duke's loyalty to the crown took many forms. A month later on 24 August he was to be found assisting Mrs Fitzherbert burn all letters relating to her secret marriage to George IV lest they fall into the wrong hands and announce the fact that the late King had married a Catholic. For several hours the Duke and Lord Albemarle fed her drawing-room fire with records of long-dead passion. 'I think, my lord, we had better hold our hand for a while', said the practical Duke at last, 'or we shall set the old woman's chimney on fire.'

Wellington was overwhelmed to be elected as the next Chancellor of Oxford University on 29 January 1834. The boyish pleasure at this unsolicited academic honour came bubbling out when he described to Harriet Arbuthnot the first installation ceremony of 7 February at Apsley House and how well he had understood the Latin. 'This shows what attention to a language for a few days will do.' Meanwhile, Grey's ministry was in a state of collapse by July 1834 after resignations over the Coercion Bill and the Poor Law. 'There exists a general uneasiness about something, nobody knows what, and dissatisfaction with everything', wrote the Duke on 5 October. (He was not against all the Whig reforms, however; he supported the Climbing Boys Bill of 1834 which forbade boys under ten sweeping chimneys.)

By November 1834 the King could bear the situation no longer. He dismissed the Whig government and summoned Wellington to rescue him, but Wellington was determined not to lead a new administration. He had promised Peel not to stand in his way or thwart the country's need for a prime minister in the Commons. It was four years since his fall from power, yet loyal service to the crown was still uppermost in his mind rather than personal ambition. He was to be caretaker until Peel formed his new Cabinet.

The death of his beloved Mrs Arbuthnot in 1834 made the Duke particularly susceptible to the charms of a Miss Anna Maria Jenkins who though only twenty had decided that the Duke's soul must be saved. On first meeting her the Duke was overcome by her beauty and seizing her hand repeated over and over again, 'Oh, how I love you! How I love you!' In alarm Anna Maria asked who made him feel thus. He had the presence of mind to reply, 'God Almighty'. She claimed to love him for his soul rather than his fame, and then set about trying to become duchess in the years that followed.

From 15 November to 9 December 1834 the Duke put into operation his own original method of caretaking. He was everybody from Prime Minister downwards, holding five major and three minor offices. Lord Grey referred to him indignantly as 'His Highness the Dictator', but in later years Wellington rather relished this description.

When Peel returned on 9 December 1834, he started immediately to assemble a Cabinet. Wellington was retained as Foreign Secretary. One of the clerks (son of Sir Walter Scott) remembered him 'of fewest words, but those few always straight to the point', writing minutes ('short and full and clear . . . [and] simple'). The new Tory party was to put forward a programme of moderate reform, as outlined in the Tamworth Manifesto. Yet it was difficult for Peel to make much impact on the statute book, because even Wellington could not protect the party from the Ultras in the Lords. The Duke sat through a 'dreadful scene' on

24 March 1835 when Peel announced his intention to resign over the Irish Tithe Bill. The bill was defeated, Peel resigned on 8 April 1835 and the Duke had held office for the last time.

William IV, 'true King of the Tories', died on 20 June 1837. At last there seemed to be an end to the deadlock between the Whigs led by Melbourne and Tories led by Peel and Wellington. Surely the young Queen Victoria's first act would be to send for the Duke? But the Duke was not surprised that she chose Melbourne. To her Wellington was simply an old hero whom her Mama had entertained now and then at Kensington. For the Duke's part he felt a protective paternal interest in Victoria's progress as sovereign. He was worried that on horseback (rather than in a carriage) she might present a target to caricaturists; he suspected she was trying to do a Queen Elizabeth at Tilbury. What was the point?

At a Buckingham House banquet on 18 July he was the only Tory present. Despite the Whig court and the charms of 'Lord M', the Tories were making overall election gains and undermining the Whig majority. Wellington was delighted with the new Tory confidence. Yet he still refused to pulverise Melbourne in the Lords over the Canadian insurrections. To the horror of the party faithful he told the House that he could not blame Melbourne personally for the inadequacy of the army in Canada. He felt no desire to toe the party line if it contradicted his own principles.

When Melbourne was finally forced to resign in May 1838 by a coalition of Conservatives and Radicals, the Queen was determined to outwit both Peel and Wellington. By the simple measure of refusing to dismiss her Whig ladies-in-waiting she prevented Peel forming an administration. The pillar of state had been overthrown. There was something peculiarly shocking in 'this mere baby of a queen setting herself in opposition to this great man, the *decus et tutamen* [glory and guardian] of the kingdom'. Wellington's retort was to make sure that Prince Albert's allowance was only £30,000 not £50,000 and to oppose his precedence over the royal dukes.

By May 1839, the Duke seemed to falter. His speeches in the House seemed paranoid and uncertain. In July he was angrily declaring: 'I have before now stood, and I can stand alone.' A stroke followed the death of his confidante young Lady Salisbury. Two remedies suggested themselves, neither very satisfactory. The zealous Miss Jenkins wanted to nurse him back to health in 1840 but he preferred to take his chances with milk of magnesia. By the end of the year he was completely recovered.

The Whigs staggered on until June 1841. Wellington's opinion was that they would only leave office 'when compelled by the police'. In true reforming spirit it was the people who compelled them rather than the police, and Peel won the election with a Conservative majority of ninety-one seats. Wellington was all set to return to political power as a member of Peel's Cabinet. By 1841 his views on reform had subtly changed. As Chancellor of Oxford he had supported reforms of the statutes governing entry to the colleges. The man who had claimed the British legislature near-perfect in 1830 was by 1837 writing sternly (about Oxford). 'There is not a Gentleman who dislikes innovation and change so much as I do. But I live in the World, I know the Times in which and the Men with whom I live. Even the best friends of the University . . . will not support the existing order of things.' He had seen the spirit of the times in a new light.

RIGHT ABOUT
FACE

What was to be the Duke's position in the new government? He was of the opinion that he could best help Peel by continuing in Cabinet as leader of the Lords, but without office. He would thus be free to deal with any trouble spots.

Peel's great experiment of 1842 was to be tariff reform and income tax. The duties on meat and corn could be lifted to help the starving and funds replenished by a new income tax – 7*d* in the £ on all incomes over £150. Wellington was more worried by the rise of Chartism than the plight of starving handloom weavers; the financial stability Peel promised would keep the menace at bay.

In Ireland there were demands for repeal of the Union. The Duke's informants – mainly government spies, Protestant parsons and Orange peers – reported frequent use among Irish radicals of the sinister phrase 'When the Day comes'. On 15 October 1845 Peel sent the dire news to Wellington: the Irish potato crop had failed. English potatoes were food; Irish potatoes were the only food. On 29 November Peel sent a memorandum to the Duke: 'Shall we modify the Corn Laws, shall we maintain it or shall we suspend it for a limited period?' Despite misgivings the Duke promised to support Peel in suspending the Corn Laws. When Peel resigned on 6 December because Lord Stanley and the Duke of Buccleuch stuck to protection, Wellington was struck by Peel's anguish at leaving Ireland in the lurch and the 'Consequences to Ireland of the Potato Disease'. Greville's account of Wellington at this time is less sympathetic: 'The Duke says "rotten potatoes have done it all; they have put Peel in his d-d fright"; and both for the cause and the effect he seems to feel equal contempt.' For the Duke, Peel's first duty had been to rescue the Queen from Richard Cobden (leader of the Chartists), if necessary by repeal of the Corn Laws, regrettable though that might be. Again Wellington's role was to support Peel and prevent mutiny in the Lords: 'A good government is more important than Corn Laws.'

It was a pleasanter duty to write pages and pages for Lord Salisbury's guidance on the management of Ireland, discussing public works, a market economy and imported maize. In private Wellington was still convinced that the party would suffer. 'I am very apprehensive that a great Mistake has been made', he wrote on 9 February 1846 to Lady Wilton. To minimise the damage, he set about converting Lord Stanley and prevent him leading a faction against Peel. He used the argument that repeal was a class issue and that the Corn Laws divided rich from poor. Although Stanley was not converted, Wellington began to be convinced by his own arguments, especially as his old friend Arbuthnot already supported the cause of free trade.

Despite Benjamin Disraeli's virulent and brilliant attacks, repeal of the Corn Laws was passed in the Commons by ninety-eight votes on 15 May 1846. In the Lords, Wellington gave a warning. Despite Stanley's continued rebellion, a bill had come up from the Commons passed by a majority there and recommended by the crown. If it were rejected the Lords would stand alone: '. . . you have great confidence in your own principles but without the Crown or the House of Commons you can do nothing'. In fact it was right about face, as Lord Clarendon had once said over emancipation – right about face with Peel or nothing. His speech had the desired effect, the Lords capitulated and the bill was passed with a majority of forty-seven. When he left the House at dawn, there were cheers from the early workers: 'God Bless you Duke.' 'For Heaven's sake people let me get to my horse.'

The fact that Wellington was known as the Iron Duke suggested he never retreated but this was entirely untrue. He had learnt from his military experiences that retreat is the safest way to advance. As the French brilliantly put it, 'reculer pour mieux sauter'. But the French retreated from Waterloo for good, not to make a new advance, whereas Wellington saw that Ireland could not be governed through coercion but might be helped towards better things by a retreat on the Corn Laws, which were popularly believed to be the cause of hunger.

Corn Law reform was the 'poisoned chalice' that brought down Peel. In revenge, the Ultra-Tories voted against coercion in Ireland. Wellington declined a place in Lord John Russell's new government but continued as commander-in-chief.

As commander-in-chief from 1842 onwards Wellington must bear a heavy responsibility for the fact the army was later unprepared to face the Crimean War. He tended to overvalue the gentlemanly side of an officer's education rather than the technical, thus undermining the training of artillery and engineers. His obsession with the country's defencelessness forbade him to experiment with new ideas and new inventions where old tried methods were available. His descendant Gerald Wellesley, the 7th Duke, has written: 'The incompetence shown during the Crimean War is often with some justification laid at his door. No man should ever cling to a job when he is too old, and no one will ever tell him when that moment arrives.'

However, in 1848, the Year of Revolutions in Europe, there was a chance for the 79-year-old Wellington to defend the monarch from another onslaught of Chartists threatening to overthrow the constitution armed with a petition of five million signatures. (Only 1,975,496 of the signatures were found to be genuine, with the Duke of Wellington's name appearing no fewer than seventeen times among the forgeries.) The Chartists lost heart, confronted by Wellington's preparations – which included 200,000 special constables. They abandoned the march on Westminster and ended up delivering the petitions by cab.

ELEVEN

THE OTHER SIDE OF THE HILL

The Great Exhibition opened at Crystal Palace in 1851. When the 82-year-old Duke tried to visit incognito, he was mobbed by 80,000 Wellington worshippers. 'Never did I . . . get such a rubbing, scrubbing and mashing . . . I expected at every moment to be crushed and I was saved by the Police alive!'

In February 1852, when the new Prime Minister, Lord Derby, read out the names of his Tory Cabinet the Duke's response to one name was 'Who-who?' and then 'Never heard of the gentleman.' To one observer at an Apsley House ball in 1852 'he seemed almost asleep'. He was impatient with admirers: a man helping him across Hyde Park Corner who was glad to assist 'the greatest man that ever lived' was told not to be a 'damned fool'. In the summer he escaped to Walmer. The gardens there were in the care of a Waterloo veteran who had once come to Wellington seeking work. Wellington had asked him if he knew anything of gardening.

'No, Your Grace.'

'Then *learn – learn*, and return here this day fortnight at the same hour. Take the place of gardener at Walmer Castle.'

'But I know nothing of gardening.'

'Neither do I.'

On 29 August he wrote jubilantly to Lady Salisbury: 'I am always well, never fatigued and I can do anything! I have none of the infirmities of old age! excepting *Vanity* perhaps!' On a visit to old Croker on 3 September he tired himself out walking from the station three miles up and down hill. He explained himself thus: 'All the business of war, and indeed all the business of life is to endeavour to find out what you do not know by what you do; that is what I called "guessing what was at the other side of the hill".' He was back at Walmer Castle in the second week of September. He climbed the castle stairs for the last time to sleep in his curtainless camp-bed with the faded green counterpane. He liked his camp-bed partly because it was his army one – only two feet nine inches wide – and partly because the sight of it had amused Mary Salisbury. She asked him how he managed to turn over in such a narrow bed and he replied: 'When it's time to turn over it's time to turn out.'

But on the morning of 14 September 1852 there was no need to turn out. Dr Hulke the apothecary left his breakfast unfinished and reached Walmer at 9 a.m. after the Duke sent summons. He was no longer conscious when Dr Hulke hurried back at 9.45 a.m. with a helper. Sitting in his favourite chair he slowly sank. At 3.25 p.m. with his son Charles and daughter-in-law Sophia beside him he died.

EPILOGUE

Wellington set the style for the great public servant of the future, single-minded and incorruptible. Tennyson's 'Ode on the Death of the Duke of Wellington' has the couplet:

> Not once or twice in our rough island-story
> The path of duty was the way to glory.

One of the Duke's peculiarities was his contempt for the press and, by extension, public opinion. This self-confidence or obstinacy was partly due to his desire to stand alone. He did not mean it in an arrogant sense of standing above any other human being; as he put it, 'I am but a man.' He was wary of reminiscences and could be persuaded to write in the margins of contemporary accounts only the words 'True' or 'False' – or merely the letters 'L' and 'DL' for 'Lie' and 'Damned Lie'.

Although devout, he hated fanaticism and abhorred the hubbub against Catholics. For instance, when Wiseman was created Cardinal, two prophets of doom wrote to him to predict the end of the world. He responded: 'I hear nothing everywhere but the dangers of popery – it is driving People mad.' When he was invited by the Orange Order to be their chief he declined with the remarkable statement that he 'couldn't join a Society which could exclude some of the most patriotic of the Queen's subjects'. His tolerance extended to other faiths. In 1839 he said: 'The whole army while I was in India, except about 50,000 men, consisted of idolaters – but they were as good soldiers as could be found anywhere.' Above all, education must never be separated from religion. Without religion you ended up with 'so many clever devils'.

Whereas friendship with clever women who could 'see what you mean', like Mrs Arbuthnot, was extremely important to the Duke in his middle years, as he grew older he found more pleasure in giving. In old age Wellington found much happiness in the friendship with Angela Burdett-Coutts, 'Miss Angela', to whom he addressed 842 letters. The Duke's letters to Miss Angela are full of telling detail even down to snippets of the Duke's 'favourite poplins' – bright and warm with no greens, blues, black or white. She proposed marriage on 7 February 1847 and received a refusal, she being thirty-two and he seventy-seven: 'You are Young, My Dearest! You have before you the Prospect of at least twenty years of enjoyment of Happiness in Life.' Together they set about rescuing fallen women by sending them to a new life in the Antipodes. When the Mendicity Society exposed some of these women as frauds, it was the society for whom the Duke expressed his dislike rather than the imposters: 'An Officer from the Mendicity Society called on me and gave me such a scolding as I have never had before in my life!'

He had a wide circle of women friends, including his daughters-in-law. He was especially devoted to the elder Lady Douro, precisely it would seem because she was childless and unloved.

The Duke's attitude to politics was that he should put country above party. Did he betray the Tory party when he allowed reform and forced the House of Lords to accept faceabout and retreat? In the dangerous years between 1830 and 1848 any violent resistance to reform would have led to revolution and counter-revolution as it did in the rest of Europe. There was no personal ambition in his politics and twice in his career, in 1834 and 1839, he refused the premiership. He spoke for the landlords of those days and that is why he initially opposed reform of the Corn Laws and the franchise, which would have introduced a new class to power – and did. His diatribe against the lower orders in 1832 must be seen in the context of the reform riots and the breaking of the windows of Apsley House.

His relationship with the army was complex. He was not a seductive leader like Napoleon. But he earned devotion from his men because they trusted him not to waste lives or guns. Yet he continued to believe that flogging was a good deterrent and insisted to the Royal Commission on Military Punishments in 1836 that Prussian reforms were not suited to the British volunteer army. In August 1846 he still believed flogging was the key to a 'disciplined army', although in the Lords that same year he declared: 'I hope I may live to see it abolished altogether.' Overall he gave the British army a tradition of victory, pride, doggedness and an iron nerve.

Wellington was compared with Marlborough by contemporaries, although he himself felt that it was impossible to make comparisons without writing a 'History of the war and the State of the Nation and of Europe at each period'. Ultimately, the comparison was always with Napoleon. Napoleon admitted that the Duke had all his qualities, with prudence added. When asked who were the greatest generals of the age, Wellington replied, according to Sir John le Couteur: 'in this age, in past ages, in any age, Napoleon'. Where Napoleon was prodigal, Wellington was economical. Wellington's stroke was a battering ram, whereas Napoleon's was the onrush of a wave, according to William Napier. But whereas Napoleon was a 'glorious tyrant', as Byron put it, creating law, education and opportunities for all, Wellington devoted himself to making constitutional government work. He lacked, perhaps, the intuitive genius of leaders like Napoleon. Viscount Montgomery in his Wellington Memorial Lecture of 1969 failed to find in him that 'inner conviction which at times will transcend reason'. Wellington's answer was recorded in Frances Salisbury's diary: he talked of inspiration coming 'like a flash of light' in an 'instant'. It was a combination of inventiveness and scientific observation, all depending on a special form of military imagination.

Wellington's sense of Britain's place in the world was essentially non-aggressive. After the Opium War in China he wrote: 'A sort of fabulous Englishman is not permitted to go about the world bullying, smuggling and plundering as he pleases.' He felt you ought to keep what you had and protect it but not make further acquisitions. Queen Victoria was taught this lesson by him.

Was he the Iron Duke? Wellington showed the army that a man could have an iron constitution without being born with it; he could acquire it the hard way. Despite bending to political reform he was generally insensitive to the spirit of the times. He was adamant that reform threatened the constitution and so had no sympathy with the liberal movements of Europe. He was suited by things as they were. Political change he disliked to his very bones. Yet he was above all a pragmatist, so he could behave as a man of iron towards reactionaries as well as towards radicals. This steely impartiality has somehow been twisted by succeeding generations, so that Wellington has been given the character of the strong silent Englishman with his stiff upper lip. That was not the Duke. As a young man he had burnt his violin in order to devote himself to the military profession. This must have been a great sacrifice – deliberately to repress the poetic and emotional side of his nature for the sake of a higher purpose.

M A P S

Maps from Elizabeth Longford, *Wellington: The Years of the Sword*, 1969, reproduced by kind permission of Weidenfeld & Nicolson.

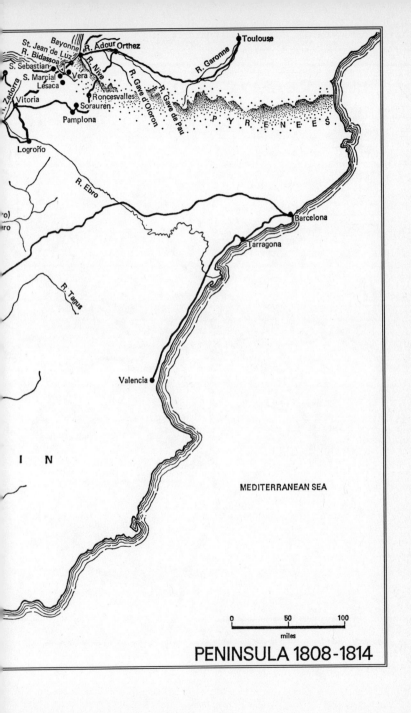

Toulouse

Bayonne
St. Jean de Luz
R. Adour Orthez
R. Bidassoa
R. Nive
S. Sebastian
S. Marcial Vera
Lesaca
Roncesvalles
Sorauren
Pamplona
R. Garonne
R. Gave d'Oloron
R. Gave de Pau
Vitoria

P Y R E N E E S

Logroño

R. Ebro

Barcelona

Tarragona

R. Tagus

Valencia

I N

MEDITERRANEAN SEA

0   50   100
miles

PENINSULA 1808-1814

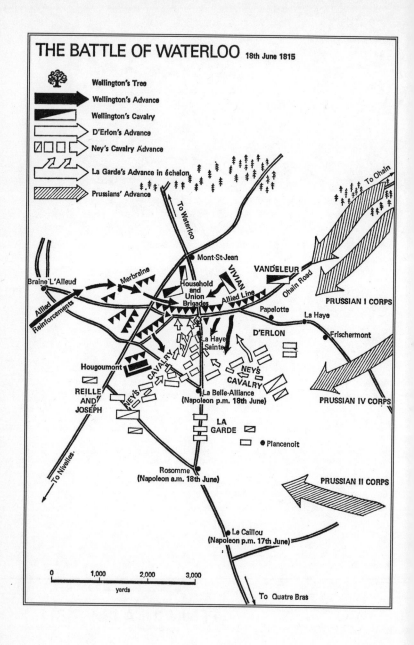

BIBLIOGRAPHY

Bryant, Arthur, *The Great Duke*, London, Collins, 1971

Fortescue, J.W., *Wellington*, London, Williams & Norgate, 2nd edn 1927

Gash, Norman, *Wellington: Studies in the Military and Political Career of the First Duke of Wellington*, Manchester, Manchester University Press, 1990

Glover, Michael, *Wellington as Military Commander*, London, Penguin, 2001

Guedalla, Philip, *The Duke*, London, Hodder & Stoughton, 1931

Hibbert, Christopher, *Wellington: a Personal History*, London, HarperCollins, 1997

James, Lawrence, *The Iron Duke*, London, Weidenfeld & Nicolson, 1992

Jupp, Peter, *British Politics on the Eve of Reform: the Duke of Wellington's Administration*, Basingstoke, Macmillan, 1998

Longford, Elizabeth (Pakenham), 2 vols: *Wellington: The Years of the Sword*, 1969, and *Wellington: Pillar of State*, 1982, London, Weidenfeld & Nicolson

——, *Wellington*, London, Weidenfeld & Nicolson, 1992 (an abridgement of the 2-vol. *Wellington* of 1969 and 1982. Also in Abacus paperback, 2001)

Neillands, Robin, *Wellington and Napoleon*, London, John Murray, 1994

Bibliography

Partridge, Michael, *The Duke of Wellington: a Bibliography*, London, Meckler, 1990

Petrie, Sir Charles, *Wellington: a Reassessment*, London, J. Barrie, 1956

Strawson, John, *The Duke and the Emperor: Wellington and Napoleon*, London, Constable, 1994

Wilson, Joan, *A Soldier's Wife: Wellington's Marriage*, London, Weidenfeld & Nicolson, 1987

QUEEN VICTORIA

POCKET BIOGRAPHY

Elizabeth Longford

Queen Victoria is the longest-reigning monarch in British history. In this concise biography, Lady Longford, long recognized as an authority on the subject, gives a full account of Queen Victoria's life and provides a unique assessment of the monarch. Victoria ascended the throne in 1837 on the death of her uncle William IV. In 1840, she married her first cousin, Prince Albert of Saxe-Coburg-Gotha, and for the next twenty years they were inseparable. Their descendants were to succeed to most of the thrones of Europe. When Albert died in 1861, Victoria's overwhelming grief made her almost retire from public life. This perceived dereliction of public duty, coupled with rumours about her relationship with her Scottish ghillie, John Brown, led to increasing criticism. Coaxed back into the public eye by Disraeli, she resumed her political and constitutional interest with vigour until her death in 1901.

ISBN 0 7509 2143 9   128pp   198 × 127mm   PB   13 b/w illustrations

A History of
the House of Lords

Lord Longford

A complex history from the Norman conquest to the present day, the book charts the waxing and waning over the years of the importance of the House of Lords. Lord Longford's account begins with a peer's-eye-view of developments introduced by the modernizing Blair administration and concludes with an examination of an unelected House of Lords in an age of democracy.

Combining history, anecdote, comment and wit, Lord Longford offers an account with a very special insight.

LORD LONGFORD (Frank Pakenham, 7th Earl of Longford) held ministerial posts in the Labour governments of 1948–51 and 1964–68.

ISBN 0 7509 2191 9   224pp   234 × 156mm   PB